Choose *Life!*

Choose
Life!

PHYLLIS OOSTERMEIJER

ISBN: 086243 602 8

Dinas is an imprint of Y Lolfa

Printed and published in Wales
by Y Lolfa Cyf., Talybont, Ceredigion SY24 5AP
e-mail ylolfa@ylolfa.com
website www.ylolfa.com
tel. (01970) 832 304
fax 832 782
isdn 832 813

I give thanks for the love of
my husband Aad,
and my three sons,
Reuben, Simeon and Matthew.
Always know that I love you.

May this book bring strength and
love to the reader.

Based on true life experiences.

1996 saw Phyllis put pen to paper.

ACKNOWLEDGEMENTS

I would like to thank Phillidar for all the help and encouragement she has given me. Our first meeting inspired me to put pen to paper.

Loving thanks to Alex – a friend in need is a friend indeed. Alex has spent hours correcting and typing my work.

C O N T E N T S

FOREWORD

PHYLLIS OOSTERMEIJER was born in Pembrokeshire. Her family – the Roch's of Molleston – farmed land around the 300 year-old Baptist chapel that had been a focal point for the supporters of Oliver Cromwell long before the 'Civil' war. A barn at Rushacre Farm was the forerunner to the chapel itself.

Since my father, Thomas Lewis Parry, was pastor at Molleston when I was born at the manse there, I have known the Roch's for as long as I've known anyone. Mrs Oostermeijer's grandparents were friends of my parents. Her father, Walter Roch, who later lived at Neyland, was a friend of mine.

Early in her life, Phyllis became a 'reciter' in chapels of all denominations, which were then still dominant influences in urban and rural life. Anniversaries and local eisteddfodau encouraged talent. The mission hall at Hazelbeach, Llandstadwell, provided an inter-denominational platform. Either there or elsewhere in the County, I heard Phyllis Roch's earliest recitations.

It follows that it doesn't surprise me that the mature Phyllis Oostermeijer has felt compelled to write this book. Much that is in it closely reflects the philosophy and teaching of the chapels and churches of Wales in their heyday.

The choice of Ella Wheeler Wilcox's poem, 'Deathless' as an introduction; the feeding-growing-reaping cycle; Alan Dromgoole's,

'Bridge Builder'; the self-examination; the discovery of 'The Savage and Beautiful Country' of Alan McGlashman and the so much more in *Choose Life!* reflect exactly the family stock and the social and communal nurturing of the writer.

What is never revealed – and as I believe never will be – is the nature of 'the Trauma' the life-shaking experience that first of all stunned and eventually inspired Phyllis Oostermeijer.

In these days of chequebook journalism and 'tell-all' tales, this book concentrates on the time beyond the difficulty.

Reaching back to the influences of her childhood, benefiting from the disciplines of her public reciting, gathering strength from the energies of the people who – over the centuries – have first looked into and then beyond themselves for inspiration in good times and in bad, Phyllis has found a way forward for herself. In her book she points the way for others.

Lord Parry of Neyland

Llangwm, Haverfordwest

Deathless

by Ella Wheeler Wilcox

There lies in the centre of each man's heart
A longing and love for the good and pure;
And if but an atom, or larger part,
I tell you this shall endure
After the body has gone to decay
Yea, after the world has passed away.

The longer I live and the more I see
Of the struggle of souls toward the heights above,
The stronger this truth comes home to me:
That the universe rests on the shoulders of love;
A love so limitless, deep, and broad,
That men have renamed it and called it God.

And nothing that was ever born or evolved,
Nothing created by light or force,
But deep in its system there lies dissolved
A shining drop from the Great Love Source;
A shining drop that shall live for aye–
Though kingdoms may perish and stars decay.

MY TREE

THIS BOOK IS LIKE A TREE. I am that tree and I need knowledge to feed my roots. With this food, I will grow strong, producing good branches on which to bear fruit. The seed of this fruit goes on to grow in other people's hearts. First, I needed enlightenment to grow, then nourishment for my roots, for the storms of life had almost blown me away and I had wilted. As a sick plant needs careful handling so I needed tender, loving care with just the right balance of food and water. Gradually I became stronger and could feel the sun's rays on my branches. Now, as a strong, healthy tree, I could produce fruit. I see this book as the seeds of my tree and want to scatter them abroad in the hope that some will grow in other people's hearts.

This book is in three parts:

Me learning, or feeding,

Me practising, or growing,

Me producing fruit for others to reap the benefits.

A complete cycle!

Some people may say, 'Well, why bother to produce anything!' For me this poem says it all:

The Bridge Builder

by Alan Dromgoole

An old man going along the highway,
Came at evening cold and grey,
To a chasm vast, wide and steep
With waters rolling deep.
The old man crossed in the twilight dim,
The sullen stream had no fears for him.
But he turned when safe on the other side
And built a bridge to span the tide.
'Old man,' said a fellow pilgrim near,
'You're wasting your strength with building here.
Your journey will end with the ending day,
You never again will pass this way.
You've crossed the chasm deep and wide,
Why build you this bridge at eventide?'
'There followeth after me today,
A youth whose feet must pass this way.
The chasm that was nought to me
To that fair-haired youth may a pitfall be.
He too must cross in the twilight dim,
Good friend, I build this bridge for him.'

How often do we recall our parents' words, or those of famous people? The thoughts that have helped me may form stepping stones for, say, my sons. They cannot know what it feels like to be my age and by the time they do, I might not be around to talk to them about it. By reading my words, they may understand feelings they have. Family traits are hard to get rid of and, who knows, in years to come our family might produce another mad person who wants to write!

Once I felt strong enough to face people again, I loved to be with those who were also walking with love in their hearts. My ears soon became attuned to picking up the vibes that genuine, caring people send out. I needed to hear positive, constructive conversation but material greed and nastiness was like poison. My wounds were still very sensitive and my nerves would react immediately to anything that had no heart in it or was not meant in a loving way.

I could not put up with stormy weather, the slightest ill wind was too much for me. Only looking back, do I realise how fragile I was. I needed to get stronger but, at the same time, I was not ready to do without protection of some kind. Fortunately, I met some truly wonderful friends while living in Spain, most of whom still keep in touch. Living somewhere like Spain meant we met people from all over the world, some on holiday and some living there permanently.

They say life gives you what you need at the right time. This was certainly the case for me - the more I sent out love the more I got back. Once you find a formula that works, you become more confident. I have always thought myself a loving person but now I wanted to explore love; was it really as powerful as I had been led to believe?

PART 1

CHAPTER 1

Why Me?

During 1990 the world that I had created for myself was turned upside-down. It was so bad we were driven to leave the country. As with so many people who go through similar suffering, we went through hell on the inside, but for folk around, who did not know us very well, we painted a rosy picture.

I've just read a book 'Why me? Why This? Why now?' That is what I asked myself. Why me? Why do I want to write this book?

I realised that it is because of my experiences. If I can help somebody to find the strength to go forward when the tide of life is low, by reminding them that it is at its lowest ebb that the tide turns, then, as one of my favourite songs puts it, 'my living will not be in vain.' If I can help just one person to find the strength to pick up the pieces and start again, like a link in a chain, who knows who the person I help will then be able to help? A strong chain is made of single links.

I'm a great believer in doing what you feel you have to do. Sometimes I get crazy ideas, like taking a rose to an old school master. If I am thinking nice thoughts about a person, isn't it better to let that person know? So many times we hold love back, thinking it is silly. So what? Be silly for once; make people smile; make people laugh! I have personally experienced great loss. Perhaps the way I found to cope will be of help to someone else. I really hope this to be true.

If the heart finds something good it usually flows over to the point where we have to tell others. When the heart is full we have to share it with someone.

I used to think I was just an ordinary person; but now I feel I am special. We are all special. We are all individuals. Nobody laughs like you, speaks like you or dances like you. What makes you laugh or cry is individual to you. You are unique and you are special.

About me and my family line

For me, not to have had any direction or real purpose in my life was terrible.

I was raised by a father and grandfather who were strong individuals, not afraid to be themselves. Characters like them are hard to find these days. Following in their footsteps, I was not afraid to stand out in a crowd. I lapped up praise. On the other hand, I didn't mind being laughed at. I stood by my actions.

Because my mother died when I was eleven, I was used to making decisions of my own early on, not wanting to trouble the aunt and uncle who were then my guardians. I would keep serious worries to myself until I could talk them over with my father.

I would have prefered to have stayed with my father but at the time this was not the done thing. Being a girl I was said to need a woman's influence. When I look at my sons I see the same strength coming through. They are not afraid to stand by their own ideas, not shy and all three are very strong characters.

They have had to learn to adapt to different circumstances. From an early age, I always told them I didn't mind what they did in life as long as they were nice people first.

My grandfather was brought up to be tough and work hard - it was a matter of work or starve. He went in for a job that he loved. He told me that he could shoe horses from morning until night and still enjoy the work. Unfortunately he had to learn farming when the demand for a blacksmith decreased.

All these thought patterns go deep and are passed on through the generations. Having the stuffing knocked out of me for a while was not very nice, but today I am so thankful to all those who helped me to regain my strength.

World Turned Upside Down

It has taken several years to understand why our world was turned upside down, and to find proof to show that we, my husband and I, were innocent.

We were happily running a nursing home that we purchased in 1989. Having been in the residential care business for many years, we finally expanded into the nursing home area.

Sinking all of our capital into what we hoped would be our final move, we were happy with the progress we were making. The nine residents who made the move with us would now have the nursing care we felt they needed. One gentleman had been with us for ten years. He was more like one of the family than a resident. Our sons had grown up with him, sharing their little ups and downs with this kindly old gent.

The business soon grew until we had thirty-two residents. This was no mean feat to achieve - it took dedication and hard graft. We had the over-all responsibility for patients and staff.

Then suddenly we found ourselves in a Catch Twenty-Two situation: the two banks we were involved with quarrelled, at least that was the understanding we had. No matter what we said or did, we could not get to the bottom of the problem. One bank told us not to worry, it was normal banking practice and all would come right. Well, all did not come right and we were stopped from trading, we lost our business and our home. Yes, you might think we should have been able to stop it. Well, not even the solicitors and barristers were able to stop it, such a tangled web was spun. We were left in total shock.

However, we can only go on telling the same story. Finally all the pieces are being put together. Vindication will be ours very soon.

In the meantime, we have been through the mill financially and emotionally. At first we did not think we would cope but thankfully we have. We learned how to make lemonade out of a lemon! The situation remained but we changed our feelings towards it. We were determined to make a new life for ourselves, one that ran alongside what we now saw as an obstacle to be overcome. It was a bitter pill to swallow but one that made us appreciate the simple things in life.

It is possible to be happy every day if we only count life's blessings and help other people. By helping another we forget our problems for a while. Keep doing this and in the end you will be so busy you won't have time to worry about the past. Of course we kept going with the bank business, but only with positive energy, never allowing a single doubt to deter us. We found a strength that, perhaps, had it not been for our unfortunate circumstances, would have remained dormant. I would like to encourage all those who are in difficulty to turn your despair into hope by making the best out of what you have. Really, it can be fun. A little imagination at times like this can produce a masterpiece. Survival brings out such wonderful hidden talent!

I learnt that when I was at rock bottom I could still lift my head and look at the sky. What wonderful advice Churchill gave to a group of students when he said, 'never, never give in!'

Try, like I do, to shut out the past and the future and make today really special. Practice this every day and soon life takes on new meaning. Start to think beautiful thoughts and beautiful deeds will follow. It costs nothing so why not give it a try!

For some time I have been wanting to tell the story of how my family and I suffered at the hands of two major banks. If I had written this in 1990, when our problems first started, I'm afraid a very different tone would have overwhelmed me. To say I was angry would be an understatement. But as the years have gone by, I have learnt to look at life in a different way. This does not take away the experiences that I had, but the way that I coped and what I have learnt has made me into the person I am today.

My life was very different before all the banking problems. I was a very happy-go-lucky person, embracing all that life had to offer me. I never envied what another person had. I was quite content to work for what I wanted. I would very often say that, 'if I never have any more than I have today I am perfectly happy.' I had found a way of life that suited me very well, I enjoyed what I was doing and it was giving me a good living. My second husband trained as a social worker, which meant he understood my business, caring for the elderly. Together we made an exceptional team. We were not afraid of hard work. I had a very nice way about me with people because I care about people. I am more humanitarian than materialistic. Although I feel passionate about a certain standard in the way I live, I will drop everything to help another person in distress.

My husband has a real flair for design. There is a lot of talk about Feng Shui these days, about balance in the home, workplace and also in the body. My husband has always had a natural tendency to do this automatically. In fact, he finds it very frustrating when things, according to his eye, are out of balance. This was great for me because I could concentrate more on the people side and he would get on with designing our business premises. We were continually commended on both areas by visitors to the nursing home, and we were regarded by East Dyfed Health Authority to be one of the top three best homes in that area. We did not find it at all stressful to produce this standard because it was an extension of how we did things for ourselves.

Thinking back, I suppose we should have been more astute regarding the setting up of business transactions. This is always easy in hindsight. At the time we gave the job to a solicitor. Not being trained ourselves, we thought this was the most sensible thing to do, and it seemed other people were doing it this way. For our accounts, we relied heavily on an accountant. Today I would not give these jobs out to someone else so readily. I know we need the services of such experts but I would keep a very close eye on whatever was being done for me.

When you first set out in business, you don't realise how green you are. I was not only running a business – I was a wife and mother as well. I had three very lively young sons and I wanted a business that would keep me at home, there for my family. At first I opened a small guest-house, which led on to caring for the elderly. This type of business gelled very well with family life. My sons benefited from having many sets of grandparents! The children brought fun and laughter into the lives of the elderly folk, which in turn kept them young. My father also spent the last years of his life living at my home, as did his father. In fact, my grandfather out-lived my father, reaching the grand age of 97. So you see we were one big happy family!

I never set out to care for the elderly. When I was at school I had the option to train as a nurse. I even spent a few days at our local County Hospital, sleeping in the nurse's quarters, just to see if I would like it. My aunt, whom I lived with, was a nursing sister and very keen for me to follow in her footsteps. However, at the time, I did not have the stomach for nursing. My experiences over those few days in a hospital did nothing to encourage me to enrole as a nurse.

My love at that time was to teach domestic science. I enjoyed cooking, especially demonstrating in front of an audience, which made me think I would enjoy teaching. As I was an only child, you would have thought I would have been encouraged along these lines, but my father was not in favour of educating a girl. So, in the end, I decided to train at a local hotel. This stood me in very good stead for the business I eventually went into.

I enjoyed the accommodation and catering industry and felt a small guest-house would be an ideal way to start off on my own. Having bought a property that belonged to my family, which was larger than we needed as a family, I decided this would be a good place to start my new business.

I'm talking about the end of the Seventies, early Eighties, timewise: the boys were growing up, Reuben my eldest was starting at secondary-school. Luckily for me, the property lay adjacent to a main road which meant I could take advantage of passing trade. I also did a few outside catering jobs until business picked up in the guest-house. Shortly after I opened, an elderly friend of my father needed to convalesce after a time in hospital and so I took my first elderly resident. I had no idea that this would open the door for the profession that took over my life.

Before the Registered Homes Act of 1984 came into force, I was actually caring for nine elderly people. During 1984 my marriage came to an end and my second husband to be came into my life. I sold that property and I moved the elderly people to a temporary address while I made new plans.

It was a huge hurdle to jump, not only on an emotional level but businesswise, because now we had to look for a property that was suitable, in order to comply with the new Registered Homes Act. At first, we rented a beautiful guest-house near St David's and that winter brought the last heavy snow we have seen in 16 years. Luckily we had a Land-Rover for transport and had great fun helping our neighbours, who were not so fortunate as ourselves.

We had a terrific local pub and on Saturday evenings a local well-known singer would play the organ and sing, encouraging all who felt inclined to join in. In Wales you don't really need to ask - as soon as a Welsh person hears music they are ready to have a sing-song! During this snowy period the lady in question was unable to drive her car and so we offered to transport her to the pub. Sharing such times forms a bond and this lovely lady eventually sang at our wedding.

Not only did we enjoy the musical evenings, we invited our 'oldies' to come along as well. Those who were able did. They were very special times with happy memories. The old men loved to sit around the log fire with a glass of stout or barley wine reminiscing about bygone days, now and again joining in with a hymn or song that they recognised. Some fine Welsh voices would end up in that pub on a Saturday night and many a good Welsh tune would bring a tear to the eye.

Being Dutch, my husband was so taken by this old-fashioned country lifestyle. He thought Wales, especially Pembrokeshire, was beautiful. After the flat land of Holland he loved the hills and valleys. Of course we're right on the coast and he wanted to see as much as he could. He never tired of finding new nooks and crannies and photographing this wonderful new life that he had found with a Welsh woman. His family would say that he was living like the Prince of Wales. We were so excited at the prospect of making our new life together.

My father's friend, my first resident, only intended to stay for two weeks. He was so weak after his operation, he hoped he would soon be well enough to return home. But for the first six months, he did not even change out of his pyjamas or dressing gown. So the weeks turned into months and eventually he asked if he could stay as a permanent resident. He liked the idea of his meals being prepared for him. He no longer wanted the responsibility of running a household. A district nurse called three times a week to change the dressing on his wound. I must admit I never really expected him to recover from the operation as well as he did, in fact, the hospital was amazed at his progress. After about six months he suddenly got up one morning and decided to get dressed and after that day he never looked back. No more dressing gown and slippers! He had to sort out the business of his house, but he was very matter-of-fact in the way he dealt with this. Once he had made up his mind that this was going to be his home he adapted so well, and enjoyed the company of other guests who stayed from time to time.

This gentleman's name was Mr Ernest Stokes and over the years he became a very well-known resident. He was a first World War veteran and he caused quite a stir when I had a Colonel to stay. The Colonel was so taken by him that he invited him to a special dinner at the Tower of

London, inviting myself as well. Because Mr Stokes felt it was such a long way to travel, and not being sure just how he would get there, he declined the invitation. On the Colonel's following visit he expressed his disappointment at Mr Stokes and myself, for not being able to come. This was news to me! Mr Stokes had not even mentioned the invitation. Apparently the Colonel had arranged a car to take us to the reception and bring us back. Once Mr Stokes realised that I knew all about it he said, 'She will never forgive me for turning such an invitation down!' I always pretended to be cross with him, a bit of fun we kept up for years!

He loved to go out in the car. In fact, it became a routine for him to join me on shopping trips, more often than not enjoying lunch in the town before returning home.

I mention such things to paint a picture of how homely I tried to make him feel and, from his reaction, I succeeded.

The social worker at the local hospital soon noticed the way Mr Stokes was being cared for. It wasn't long before I was asked to take another gentleman and then a lady and so on and so on. Within a short time I found I was caring for nine elderly people. They were on a pension similar to staying in a residential hotel. It was all very relaxed and homely.

Then, one day in 1984, a gentleman called at my door and informed me that a new act was coming into force regarding caring for the elderly - the Registered Homes Act 1984.

As I have already stated, we went on to be successful in the care of the elderly. Then we hit an iceberg, so to speak, causing my family and I to be shipwrecked in Spain. I cried for three months, my husband was very concerned and spoke to my sons about his fear that I would never get over this.

Hence the scene, which became the turning point for me:

So How did I Turn Things Around?

A turning point came while I was sitting on a beach in Spain. I was feeling so depressed and miserable. Then my fifteen-year-old son pointed out that as I couldn't do a thing about my problems, I might as well stop dwelling on them, and that I should try to enjoy the day and what was around me, instead of wishing for something I couldn't have. It hit me like a rock. Yesterday's unhappiness didn't have to be carried with me for ever. Each day is brand new and unfilled. Why fill it up with yesterday's misery? I should try to be happy one day at a time. I began to feel ashamed of the way I had been feeling, and with determination, decided to look forward instead of backwards. When you realise that you have hit rock bottom then you are already on the way up.

Having left my homeland of Wales and sought sanctuary in Spain, not because I wanted to but because we were advised that this would be a good thing to do at that time, I was without my regular network of friends. Not wanting to share my problems with strangers, I set about finding a survival package for myself.

I found a second-hand bookshop in the little town of Nerja. It had a very good English section because many British people were settling in that area. I found a book by Diana Cooper, Light Up Your Life, which encouraged me to look within for the key to a successful and happy life-style.

I returned to the second-hand bookshop, and found a book about a man on a journey in Turkey. It was called The Last Barrier and it impressed me so much that I searched for more helpful books.

Notes on The Last Barrier

Who ever has heared of me, let him prepare to come and see
me, who ever desires me, let him search for me, he will find
me, then let him choose none other than I.
        –Shami-I-Tabriz

Once I started to read this book, it was almost impossible to stop. Like Reshad Field, I too was searching for a lifeline. This book had not come to me by chance. I felt excited by every word I read. At the time of reading, Reshad's healing work meant nothing to me, but now as my husband is a REIKI healer, on subsequent readings his healing work stands out.

It is said, once the pupil is ready the teacher appears. Miraculously, signposts appear directing us to the source of information needed. Reshad often had set backs and was amazed whenever plans worked out, thinking circumstances had brought him to that point, only to be reminded that there was no such thing as chance. Was he being guided? I was fascinated and wanted to know more!

He was told all of mankind are connected by an invisible thread. Whatever is said or done in one place has an effect everywhere else in the world. But the degree of effect is dependant on our level of awareness. Are we tuned in? This must be why collective prayers sent out for, say, healing can and do have great results.

Energy Follows Thought

Believing that to be true, I was prepared to take time to be quiet, ready to let messages and healing come to me.

I love this quote from The Savage and Beautiful Country by Alan Mc Glashan.

Delight is the secret. And the secret is this: to grow quiet and listen, to stop thinking, stop moving, almost to stop breathing, to create an inner stillness in which like mice in a deserted house, capacities and awareness too wayward and too fugitive for every day use may delicately emerge.

Reshad became aware that until you understand the omnipotence of God, you will always think you are the cause of something. In my own strength, I was not doing very well. Once I surrendered myself to the energies of the universe a new sense of purpose flowed through my veins. I could feel life returning, similar to that feeling you get when pins and needles wear off and you can feel your fingers again. I had lost the joy of life. I was stuck in the past!

We have to leave the past behind, free ourselves from old worries, tie off any loose ends, go forward freely. I was desperate for knowledge, thinking to cram as much in as possible. Now I realise this will be given at the right time. Education comes from the Latin word educare, which means to bring forth.

Quote

> Soul receives from soul that knowledge, therefore not by book nor from tongue. If knowledge of mysteries come after emptiness of mind, that is illumination of heart.
> –Melana J Elauddin

In our search we must be prepared to make mistakes, and not be afraid to say so – or show the result of such mistakes. Let the scars of the heart be seen, for by their scars are known the men who are in the way of love. By being honest we will attract respect from our fellow human beings.

Reshad was also taught that the awareness path requires conscious suffering. Remember that the rosebush can produce a perfect rose only through correct pruning. Don't be surprised if at some point you get totally confused by it all. Often the word DOUBT would come into my mind. This is a word we don't want to dwell on. It means to hesitate; waver; be uncertain. Don't give up!

Maybe you are on the awareness path because of a rejection of some sort, searching for something better, more pure.

The Last Barrier captures what I was feeling, powerless to get myself out of the situation I was in. Reshad was told it was at such moments that we draw near the beginning of the path of knowledge; and with such words of wisdom the book opened up for me.

I leave you with the Epilogue:

> Reason is powerless in the expression of love. Love alone is capable of revealing the truth of love and being a lover. The way of the prophets is the way of Truth. If you want to live, die in love, die in love if you want to remain alive.
> —Mevlana Jelau'ddin Rumi

We are all individuals – maybe something else will be the trigger for you.

My Search Continues

My problems did not fly away overnight; the depressions came in waves, but in-between I felt that I was doing something positive to change my frame of mind.

Along with the reading of books, I found I was starting to talk to people. I was amazed to find how many people are going through difficult times or have been through them. I found people with bigger problems than I had, or should I say, different problems, because for me what I had to cope with filled my life. It doesn't always make you feel better to hear of someone with twice as many problems as you have, not when you are trapped in yours.

When the dark clouds start to lift and you begin to see more of the landscape, then it gradually becomes possible to put problems into perspective. But it doesn't happen all at once.

Whenever I felt a low coming, on I would reach for a book. If the book had relaxation exercises in it, I would try to practise them. If it was about visualisation techniques, then I would see myself in a place that I loved as a child. I would think of happy things.

It was not easy. I had never done such things before. The more I persevered the easier it became.

I started to use relaxation tapes and I found they helped enormously. The company of the voices on the tapes made me feel I was not alone. After reading many books, and putting into practice what I read, I realised I was making definite progress.

When I let go of my unhappiness and decided that I wanted to go forward, the first thing I learnt to do was to accept my situation. At first I did not want to believe it had happened to me, let alone accept it. But eventually I realised that I was fed up of carrying it around with me. Of course it had happened and I felt I had every right to be angry about it. But I also came to know that the time had come for the terrible anger to stop.

So what if it had spoiled the life I had enjoyed? I was the one spoiling my life now by keeping this anger with me. I was damaging myself by holding onto it. It was becoming a crutch, and a barrier to the changes I now wanted to make.

Somehow I had to let it go and heal the hurt. Love is the great healer. But how could I achieve that? The next step had to be forgiveness.

Could I forgive those who I thought were to blame for my situation? I decided I would try. I had to work out a way of dealing with the grudges I felt against the people I held responsible. How could I do this?

For me letters were the answer. I was too far away to be able to visit people face to face, and even if it had been possible I think I would still have written to most people. I was trying to be strong and brave, but I wasn't feeling all that brave inside. But this was something I really wanted to do.

So I poured my heart out in letter form. It was hard to tell people you now forgave them in the hope that they would forgive you in return. Past deeds can come between good relationships. Things done in haste, things done for whatever reason, mostly material greed, lead us to lose dear family and friends. Once I got everything off my chest and did all that was possible to do, I then turned to things that were not so easy to sort out.

When there was no particular person to speak to or write to, it was difficult to know what to do. So, to resolve these situations, I would place each problem in a bubble. Then I would imagine it floating away from me. As I watched it go, I knew that if ever I saw a chance to do something about it, I could always burst the bubble and sort it out then.

It was a wonderful way to give my mind a spring clean and remove worrying thoughts from within. Once we kick old things out, it makes way for the new. And I wanted the new so badly. I was beginning to feel that life was for living again.

When I was young, I just set out with arms wide open to embrace whatever life had to offer, not expecting the knocks I received to hit me so low. Now, slowly, I was reaching out again, but this time trying to prepare myself for uneven ground. Sometimes we get the knocks we ask for, by not being aware enough of what is going on around us. We fall time and time again until we have to listen.

The First Positive Step

I call warnings 'whispers'. How often have we wondered why something is happening and then dismissed it, blindly carrying on regardless.

Suddenly, something terrible happens. If only we had listened a bit harder and acted on the whispers. If only we could stop and take stock. If we took the time to ask ourselves, 'Is life trying to tell us something? If so, what?' If your car is making a strange noise, it is wise to look for the cause of it. If we ignore it, who knows what might happen next?

If family or friends get mad at you, could it be they are mad with themselves? Find the time to talk to them. If you feel you haven't done anything – say so. Don't let it build up. Try to get the thorn out before the pus starts forming.

Always listen to life's whispers. Try to keep your wits about you and be aware of what is happening. This can be a very powerful warning system. If we can take the heat out of a situation before it becomes a crisis, how many less letters we shall need to write. I have been putting this into practice ever since that time and it really works. Now I find I am picking up other people's whispers and I do try to explain them. Sometimes I get a good response, other times not – but now I do speak out in the hope that it will do some good.

If you see a child about to run in front of a car you almost break your neck to stop him. So it is when you sharpen your wits. More and more, you pick up whispers. As long as we wrap up our help with sincere love, it cannot fail. Love will win when all else fails.

Having surrendered to my situation, I now felt it was time to be honest with the folk who really meant something special to me. This was hard because who wants to put dirty washing out for all to see?

It was not easy, but for family and friends to understand what was happening to me, I needed to be honest with them. After all, this was my life and, whether I liked it or not, this was real and was happening to me. By being more honest with myself and with my family and friends, it gave them the courage to be more honest with themselves and with me. Facing up to the situation gave me a new-found courage and, by telling my story, I found that some of them were also able to find the courage to release their hidden fears. It had a knock-on effect.

I felt I was living two lives. On the outside, pretending things were not as bad as they were, I kept hoping things would get better and there would be no need to admit anything. We can sometimes fool ourselves with this attitude, and the more we cover things up, the harder it becomes to uncover them. Inside our shell we create hell, depression, withdrawal, not wanting to reach out or confide in anyone, finding it too painful to tell the truth.

This prevents us from making new friends, real friends, because we can never let our real self show any more and people find it hard to relate to what they can't see.

I was making myself ill with this façade. I had always loved truth, always insisted my three sons be truthful, and yet here I was presenting a false face to the world.

I was pretending to be something I wasn't and hating myself for it.

But, step by step, I found a way out. I love the story about the two frogs in a bucket of milk. One was an optimist, the other a pessimist. After swimming for quite a while the pessimist felt he would never get out, so he stopped swimming and drowned. Meanwhile the optimist kept going. Eventually he found he was floating on a pat of butter and could easily jump out. The moral is never give up. When the going gets tough and you think you are beaten, that extra effort can find you a way out. At this point I told the truth to my family. I tried to be discerning concerning older members, in case it upset them.

Naturally it did not affect everyone in the same way. Some felt my pain more than others. But for me, it was a great weight lifted from my mind. I could now write honest letters. I could be me again.

Try to get started with pen and paper. Do it today. Do it now. Don't say to yourself, 'Oh I want to do that.' Instead say, 'I am doing it now.' Never put off until tomorrow what you can do today. There is only one way to find out if something works and that is to try it, prove it to yourself.

Resentment and anger that is kept inside can, in time, eat away at the body, causing illness. We cause our own body to suffer. Don't swallow your anger, learn to express it. Don't be self-righteous, too proud to ask for or give forgiveness.

It will free us, unblock the system, keep us healthy. If we or others have made mistakes, remember no blame should be attached. We all have to learn. Sometimes we make mistakes, not because we set out to do wrong, but when we set out to do our best.

It is said that if you don't make mistakes you don't make anything. It is good to give the mind a spring clean and once we recognise the problems and do our best to solve them, we can fill the space with love and good purpose so that the worries and fears cannot get back in.

For me this was the first positive step.

The Second Positive Step

Once the unblocking starts, the energy starts to flow. Suddenly my home seemed a mess. I wanted to make everything look uncluttered. I looked at the broken items and wondered what I was keeping them for! So out they went. There were all those plants that looked half dead – if they could not be made cheerful, out they went. We all know how rubbish builds up in drawers and cupboards. I found I now had the energy to sort things out and throw the rubbish away. The same with my clothes. If I had not worn a garment for ages, or things no longer fitted – out they went.

Nothing needs to be wasted now that we have so many charity shops and you know you are doing some good as well. I learnt that once you make things move in your life, parting with the old makes room for the new to come in. By getting rid of old clothes we make room for new ones. We start this flowing process. The same with make-up, old creams and powders not used for ages – get rid of them, let them go and try something different.

It is always exciting when we go somewhere for the first time. So it is with new clothes and make-up, or aftershaves and perfumes. Say to yourself, I am going to do this. I do deserve this for myself. For me to throw things out was terrible. I always kept things for a rainy day. Well, the rainy day came and they were no use at all. The less we clutter up our lives the freer we become. This was my experience. I found that a great weight lifted off my mind, and with it, my confidence started to build up again.

One of the worst effects of bad knocks is when we loose confidence and are afraid to try again. But if we can recognise what is happening, we CAN get over that. It is sometimes hard to remember that the body is designed to be fit and healthy and the mind is designed to be happy and full of the joy of life. Why stop that joy flowing through our veins?

With each positive step we make we will feel confidence returning. Along with confidence comes happiness. Happiness is like the sunshine; it brings the flowers into bloom. We can't turn on sunshine on demand. But we can enjoy it, however fleetingly, when it shines. What a pity to ignore even little patches of it. By cultivating sunshine thoughts in our minds and hearts, more and more will be reflected in our actions.

The moment we realise we have hit rock bottom and we want to do something about it is a very tricky time.

One part of us could easily let it all go. How on earth are we going to cope? Can we ever face reality again? It is a steep hill to climb. If we make the first step, that is such a positive move.

Remember, to do something is better than doing nothing, and standing still can end in sliding backwards. But once we make a new move, we are opening ourselves up for new experiences.

Simple things like a different make of toothpaste, soap, or shampoo. Try scrambled eggs instead of cereal and toast. If you take a walk turn right instead of left. There are so many variations to be had in this world.

Don't wait for a neighbour to smile and say hello, try being the first to do it. See today as the first day of the rest of your life – be determined to do something different. Change your hairstyle, drink black coffee instead of white. Make your senses aware of different tastes and smells. Really listen to what is being said. Try to lose yourself in what is going on around you. It is amazing how quickly you will start to find yourself again.

For me the upward climb was hard and tears were never very far away. Now I can honestly say the crying bouts have stopped. Anyone who has ever experienced such crying spells will understand what I'm talking about. You really believe your whole world to be in threads. Keep climbing up that hill – with each step you will find a hand waiting to help. Reach out and take the help. I always felt too embarrassed to ask for help, but not any more.

A Thought

The whole crux of writing this book was to bring over this one thing. In giving in to this universal energy, God, Higher Spirit, whatever you like to call it, we are able to do all that is inside of us, all we really want to. It sounds contradictory – giving in to another's will, you would think you would loose yourself. But this works in the opposite way.

Maybe all we are really doing is giving in to our better self. We are all powerful and we are all there is. All I know is once I let life bring things to me it opened up a new strength inside of me. They say seek and you will find. A lot of self-help books speak about the power within. Yes, we have the power to experience much more than the majority of us think or do. If, for instance, you have the feeling you would love to play the piano, well, do it! Life will help you. Take the first step and trust that life will give you the lessons, the piano, and it will. Go into music shops, talk to people in that world and you will be surprised how quickly you will reach your goal.

It is funny to think of me writing a book. For years I sent off to writing schools for courses, but I didn't join. I wanted to. What stopped me was my lack of trust in myself that I could do it.

I love writing letters, keeping little accounts of funny things that have happened in my life. You see, it was there all the time, waiting to come out. Maybe you are like that, and have something you really would like to do or somewhere you really want to visit.

Visualise it and start doing something about it. You know what I'm talking about. Search within yourself.

Realistic Steps

Don't set aims too high at first. I once read, 'don't think of flying to the moon unless that is what you really want.' Take small steps to begin with and see the road stretch before you. You never know what is around the next corner. How many times have you looked at other people and wished you could be like them? Well, you can, but not as them, as you. Rome wasn't built in a day, as we are always being told. Of course it wasn't. Think about these sayings, they have encouraged others before us and they can tell us a lot.

Listen to the words of songs. Somebody felt those words. One line can change our path, once we stop and really listen, listen to the reaction the words have on us.

When you are in a depressed state, know that the power is within you to get out of that situation. When all seems lost, don't rely on doctors or family and friends to save you. You have to pull yourself up by your boot laces and you can and will do it. If I can do it, anyone can.

How Adversity Can Help

I remember reading a little talk my mother had written for a sisterhood meeting. She spoke about a husband and wife who were quarrelling and fighting at home. It had got so bad there was a possibility that they would part. Then their young son became critically ill and was taken to hospital.

They spent days by his bedside, pulling together, giving all their love and strength in the hope it would help save their little boy. Realising how precious he was to them, the things they had been fighting about appeared trivial. Slowly the boy began to get better and eventually recovered. Did the parents go on fighting? No, they pulled together, giving more love to each other than ever before.

It might have gone the other way, but it was obvious that this was what they wanted deep down. It took a tragic situation to make them stop and think.

The lesson came at the right time but was it a coincidence? Did the child pick up the tension from his parents, affecting him emotionally, and resulting in his illness? If my words and actions could have such an emotional effect as to cause physical illness, I felt I should be more conscious of what I was giving out to others.

Cast your bread on the waters and it will return tenfold to you. If what you give out is given with love, not hatred or anger, it will return to you tenfold.

Not always an easy thing to do. Another saying tells us that, 'The heart never runs empty from loving nor the purse from giving.' Try living it. It works for me, although things do not always return from the direction you expected. That is not important. The invisible channels that go between us see to it that we get back what we give out. Try a simple smile, it costs nothing. Try giving it away to a group of people and see how many smile back.

Give what you can when you can, give it freely and be glad you have it to give away. You will be surprised what life gives back to you. Maybe then you will draw towards you all that your heart desires.

By getting rid of an old pattern of life, that maybe brought us to where we are, we will make room for the new. It is exciting! Try it today. Find something that you have that you can well do without and give it away, or sell it so that someone else can find joy in it. By selling things we keep things flowing. You don't have to give everything you don't need away, if you can turn it into money energy, do so. See it as an exchange. That is what life is giving you back for parting with it. If this all sounds too simple, just try it before you make your mind up.

Worry is a waste of energy. What we worried about ten years ago, we do not even remember today. Did worrying ever do you any good? Forget it.

Thinking the grass is always greener is also a waste of energy. It might look green, but it is just as hard to cut! Start from where you are, appreciate what you have and stop wasting energy on what you haven't got.

If you don't have a washing machine, as we didn't in Spain, be glad you have hands and the strength to wash by hand. It might even be better for you, giving you exercise for your body. Instead of sitting there depressed and wringing your hands, try wringing some clothes.

No money for writing paper? Make some. You can use any blank paper you come across. Maybe you can pick up leaflets advertising a forthcoming event. Write a little note on the back. Maybe a friend would be glad you brought the notice to his/her attention.

One friend I have keeps his building invoices to write notes on. It makes me laugh because I think, he's building something with bricks. Or painting again, if the invoice is for paint. We are setting up our own recycling programme. Anything that comes to me in the post I see if I can reuse.

I always cut the fronts off pretty cards, birthday, Christmas, or cards sent as letters, and reuse them as post cards, providing the other side has not been written on.

I have even cut out pretty pictures from magazines and stuck them onto plain paper to make my own cards. This method of saving what we are given can be carried out throughout the home. You can turn jars and plastic containers into all sorts of useful things. This saves money, helps to save resources on the planet, and keeps us busy when we are recovering from a difficult period in our lives.

Maybe you will find your artistic side. Who knows where that might lead.

CHAPTER 2

Money

For whatever reason we find ourselves having to manage on a reduced income – be it through illness, redundancy, financial problems, divorce or when we are just starting out to earn our own living – the sooner we face the situation the better. Don't be an ostrich with your head in the sand. It won't go away on its own.

Major Re-adjustments

Remember the way around a problem is through it. Lay your financial income and expenditure on the table, so to speak. Take a good look at everything and then make a list of essential expenses, that is, what you need to keep body and soul alive. It is essential to get your priorities in order.

If you have never had to think too much about such things before, this might sound very simplistic but it is absolutely necessary if you are to survive a difficult patch, or, perhaps, a substantially longer period. (Mine turned into years.)

Take accommodation for instance. Can you afford to pay for it? Maybe, like me, you have never had to face this before. If you do find yourself in such dire straits, having previously taken your home for granted, this can be an enormous problem. You only have to walk the streets of any large city or town to see this firsthand.

One lady, once a renowned actress, who had suffered one repeated illness after another, found her finances ruined by medical bills and, not well enough to work, ended up sleeping in a cardboard box in an unsavoury neighbourhood. Trying to cover up her embarrassment, she joked, 'I'm not from this part of town,' only to be told, 'None of us are.'

If this happens to you, first enquire of family or friends. They may be able to help with accommodation for a short time until another solution can be found.

There are many other possibilities once this initial pressure is lifted. For example, are you eligible for housing benefit? Once the boundaries are clear then you are more able to search in the right places. No good looking for pearls on the top of a mountain!

See this as a temporary situation and always be ready to move on when the time is right. While exploring every avenue you might be pleasantly surprised by what you find. By positive actions and trusting that life has something in store for you, a way will be found.

You might have a limited knowledge of what accommodation is available but, by speaking to people who deal with this on a daily basis, you will gain information, helping you to make the best choice.

All of a sudden, you see material needs from a different angle. This is now survival and you must get your priorities right. Ditch everything that might drag you under. To live to tell the tale is all that really matters.

Nobody likes to sacrifice standards – it can be hell – but the funny thing is, what may be sometimes forced upon you, can turn out to be a better way of life. Not richer in a materialistic sense but a more joyous way of living.

Actually, we need very little to keep the body alive. Again it's only when life forces us to take stock that we are prepared to change. Many factors prevent this otherwise – we worry what other people might think. There's media pressure. Do we ever stop and think what we would really like and take positive steps to bring that about?

Not often, I think, and even then we dismiss it as fanciful. There are so many wonderful, pleasurable things that can enrich our lives and don't cost a penny. Watch a sunset, walk on a beach, climb to the top of the hill and let the view fill your very soul. When did you last do one of these things?

As long as your income provides what is needed to stay alive, nature can compensate in abundance for what is needed to satisfy the heart and mind.

I digress a second. My father always used to say we have two hearts, one of flesh and blood and the other of emotions. We say 'good-hearted people', 'dying of a broken heart', 'have a heart-to-heart talk' and 'lovers want to give each other their hearts'.

How can we nourish this other heart? Take time to find out what condition yours is in.

We can allow a difficult situation to get us down, thus causing stress, or we can say, 'Away with this, I'm going to sort things out!' This response can stop stress getting a foothold.

Once we sort our accommodation out, it is surprising what peace of mind it will bring. Just to have this peace of mind will warrant making material sacrifices. Making the old pennies go around is not easy. I saw a television programme the other day, it pointed out that if we thought twice, we would probably cut our spending in half.

Do we really need a new jumper? How many hours of labour will be needed to purchase the one we like? Can we find a cheaper one that will serve the same purpose? Do we really need it or are we comfort-buying? Do we need it now or can we use the money for more essential things?

We can't wear six jumpers at the same time. A friend of mine told me that he often comfort-buys, buying as many as six shirts at once, only to find that he wears two or three, while the others are left hanging in the wardrobe for ever.

Even when times are better, it is far nicer to ring the changes each season. Try selecting three co-ordinating outfits, things you really like, and wear them as much as you like. How often do we keep our favourite clothes for 'best' and in the end they are too small or outdated? Then we are sorry we didn't wear them more often.

I learned the hard way about letting material things go. I remember my husband would ask, 'What can we sell?' This would hurt. I hated parting with what I had gathered around me. Then I realised our bodies are more precious. If there has to be a choice between eating or keeping something to look at, it must be survival. When times improve, it is amazing how quickly we accumulate material possessions. Once we experience living with fewer things, nine times out of ten we like it very much and continue to do so.

The more worthwhile something is, the less value we place on it. So a priest makes a pittance and a striptease dancer a fortune. We say filthy rich. If we think money is bad and we are good. Hey Presto! Conflict. Most people do what they hate for a living thus justifying the payment they receive for it. You would rather starve than take filthy money for pure service, if the service loses its purity you take money for it! That is one reason our money comes in fits and starts with no clear focus. The thoughts we send out come back, therefore we have to change our thinking and I couldn't put it better than Neale Donald Walsh, *Conversations with God.*

Thought – word – deed. Bless money as it comes to you for with the money bills are paid. Bills come from items of energy used – electricity, water, etc. What are we worth? Earn what you need in order to pay for what you use, no longer thinking money is dirty. Like a computer, you can buy a programme or make your own, start modifying any thoughts that conflict with your complaints. If you do not have enough money maybe it is time to upgrade the thoughts we have about money. Another thought, maybe money is not the real problem but what we now spend it on and what happiness is it bringing us. Food for thought!

If you see someone truly in need, maybe your first instinct is to give generously, money, time, whatever. Act quickly on that thought before your old thought countermands it. To change our situation or attitude takes action but, of course, we will experience teething problems. A new pair of shoes feels different! Persevere in spite of adverse old thoughts, after all the way brought you to this point. Look at past experiences, do you really want to keep repeating them? If 'no' is the answer, you must be brave enough to try the reverse action.

One day my husband thought he was repeating an old mistake so, immediately, he stopped himself in his tracks and said, 'No.' That was the end of it but, if he had dithered, history would probably have repeated itself. So it makes sense to go quickly the opposite way; the proof of the pudding is in the eating.

Sometimes, when I'm laying in bed, a whole story comes into my head. I know if I just lie there and expect to remember it the next morning, it will have gone, so I need to act straight away. I grab a pen and paper and make notes as experience has taught me this. To make the most of my ideas, I had to change.

CHAPTER 3

Health

W hen our bodies show signs of nutritional neglect, a good balanced diet usually corrects the disorder. So too with our emotional needs. Once an unloved child or adult is given love or a lonely person has company, those wounds are able to heal. A balance of the physical and emotional will make us whole again.

Depression

Depression can be brought about by unhappy circumstances, such as a broken love affair, loss of a loved one, a debilitating illness or redundancy. Once we can accept these circumstances and are prepared to build that part of our lives back again, it is reasonable to expect the depression to lift.

When depression is brought about by mood swings, hormone levels may be unbalanced. This needs to be looked at from the inside out rather than look for outside influences causing stress. Once we are under stress it is difficult to see things in a reasonable way. Simple everyday problems become distorted and this is usually caused by the inability to take any more stress – it's like every nerve cries out, 'Stop, I can't take anymore!' At these times never be too proud to ask for help. Talk to family and friends and, once the reason is established and the right treatment started, slowly you will be able to take more and more responsibility again.

If you think your hormones could be out of balance, have a good M.O.T. from the doctor. Learn as much about the workings of your body as possible. Then get a good routine going. If you need to take regular medication, draw up a daily plan and stick to it. If you need to reduce your fat intake, be conscious of this fact. If you know exercise is your downfall, try to work on that. Tighten up all aspects of your life. It will result in a healthier you, inducing peace of mind.

Take a diabetic, for instance. It would be no use taking an insulin injection every other day if you need a daily dose! Learn to be your own mechanic and get to know your wonderful body. It will give good service in return. Checking car tyres regularly might prevent a serious accident. So too with our bodies. An ounce of prevention could save a pound of treatment.

If our present situation is not working, for whatever reason, what harm can it do to take a good hard look at ourselves? Many well-known names in Personal Development have written extensively about the connections between the mind and physical functioning. The power of the mind, and positive states such as hope and joy, to effect bodily changes is a major theme of healing literature, where stories abound of people who have healed themselves of serious diseases like cancer.

Whilst we were living in Spain we met a couple that had changed their lifestyle completely by moving from Britain to Spain after the husband had undergone a major operation for cancer. His wife told me that he had not been back for any check-up appointments, or even spoken the word 'cancer' since that time.

They had bought a small farmhouse with a few acres of land where orange and lemon trees grew, and enjoyed the weather of the Costa Del Sol. His attitude was very positive, and it seemed to me he had taken responsibility for how he was going to live his life – enjoying life in the present rather than dwelling on the past. His serious illness had prompted him to take steps towards living a life, that maybe he had previously only dreamed about – when I met him he was a picture of good health and he radiated contentment!

Obviously this man no longer wanted to live his former lifestyle, which had brought him to physical illness. His wife told me that he was convinced that his change of environment had halted his illness. Whether this was so, or if it was the result of his surgery, or a combination of both did not seem to matter to him. He had enjoyed ten years of good health in 'paradise'. Positive thinking was well and truly working for him! We don't just want to survive. A little happiness is not too much to ask for. So be prepared to make the necessary changes if this would result in, not only more happiness, but better health. What are we waiting for!

I used to think 'Oh, I can't do that!' Now I look at people around me and I think that if they can do it, so can I. The men and women who rocket off to the moon are flesh and blood just like me. Everything becomes possible once you know how.

Those brave ones amongst us, those with the pioneering spirit, really push back existing boundaries. If you feel strongly enough about something, you too can achieve wonders. If we see ourselves as healthy and strong, that is how we will start to feel. But if we keep telling ourselves we are ill and weak, that is how we will feel. We can talk ourselves into not doing something because we feel under the weather, but look at the flipside. How many times have you camouflaged a cold because you really wanted to go somewhere? The joy you experience overrides the illness.

Some types of depression will require hospital treatment but the majority who suffer from anxiety and mood swings are treated by G.P.s. Usually the outward symptoms are treated but I urge you to find the cause. Work on that and you will find the symptoms disappear.

As I have already written, an inner imbalance as seen, say, in the blood, can be treated but at the same time we must take stock of our present lifestyle. Can we find a reason for this happening, thus preventing this same problem from developing again?

I remember a lady who was visiting a healer saying she lived for these visits, thinking the healer would miraculously heal her, but she slowly realised the healing has to come from herself.

The cure is not within a healer but within ourselves. The illness is within ourselves and so is the cure. Of course we need medical and holistic treatment but, if we choose not to get better, we won't.

As I write this, there are so many folk not so fortunate as ourselves. That is not to say we do not have our bag of troubles but we are blessed with the knowledge of how to find the strength to sustain us. Knowledge brings wisdom or awareness and we should feel privileged that we can work out a solution. It should radiate from us.

Whenever we come up against a problem, we can face it, deal with it and trust the greatest spirit of all to see us through. As though we have been treated with Scotch Guard, a protective coating has been added. Instead of fearing problems, we are free to spread light and hope to others. I am a great believer in sharing what good fortune we have found with other people. Hold your candle up for everyone to see. Like the song, 'this little light of mine, I'm going to let it shine, let it shine all the time...'

How to Add Years to Years

I have been with my husband since 1984 and the one thing that puzzled me was the catnaps he took every day. I used to think, My, he needs a lot of sleep! But now I understand it is not sleep so much as relaxation. He does automatically what the majority of us could do with learning.

Did you know that Winston Churchill was able to work sixteen hours a day even when he was over sixty because he took three rest periods during the day? Because he rested frequently, thus preventing fatigue, he was able to work on fresh and fit.

In Daniel W. Josselyn's book Why Be Tired he wrote, 'Rest is not a matter of doing absolutely nothing... Rest is repair.'

Rest has a knock-on effect because it relaxes the mind and body, which repairs physical illnesses. Those who practice this see a marked difference emotionally, causing them to worry less.

Clinical tests show that any nervous or emotional state disappears during complete relaxation, which means you cannot worry if you relax!

Prevention is always better than cure, so why not learn to prevent fatigue by resting before you feel tired?

The only way to prove this is to try it for a month; research shows by resting more we are able to work harder. Employers would do well to heed this: rest periods are important.

By resting more we will produce more of whatever we do, prevent worry and illness, which in turn should earn us a longer life span.

What Makes You Tired?

Believe it or not, scientific tests showed that mental work alone can't make you tired. They discovered that blood passing through the brain, when active, shows no fatigue at all, but blood taken from a labourer while he was working was full of 'fatigue toxins'.

Still, we do get tired with mental work because emotions come into play. Emotions can cause tension which affects the muscles. Hard work alone can be overcome by a good night's rest, but anxiety and worry do more harm.

When we sit to do mental work we hunch up our shoulders, tensing our muscles, so what is the answer? One word: RELAX.

Learn to relax in everything you do. Be aware of the feeling in your body. If you feel the muscles tensing make a conscious effort and relax. We can cultivate good habits as well as bad – for a few minutes stop what you are doing, close your eyes and let your body go limp. Feel the difference, say the word RELAX, repeat it over and over.

Look out for odd moments that you can relax. Whenever possible stretch out on a couch or even lay on the floor. Ten minutes of this out of a lunch break will pay huge dividends.

It is very useful to think of a cat when you need to relax. The wise old yogis in India say that if you want to master the art of relaxation, study the cat.

Worry!

Sometimes our worries prevent us from relaxing. A good old-fashioned trick which works wonders is to find someone you can trust and talk your troubles over... a trouble shared is a trouble halved!

By talking we confront our problems and very often find answers that were there all the time but tension kept us from seeing them.

So who can we turn to? A friend or a relative. We used to be able to talk to our family doctor, but these days they are so busy. What about a priest or member of the local Church, or one of the many alternative therapists?

Just to talk can be so healing, dispersing tight knots in the body.

This and regular rest periods will enable us to cope better and enjoy a healthier, happier life.

Things to Practise

Relax the body whenever possible.

Catnap throughout the day.

Make time to relax completely at least once a day – lay on a couch, bed or the floor.

Talk your worries over with someone you trust.

Instead of dwelling on the shortcomings of others, try thinking of uplifting things ... read a beautiful poem or quotation.

Exercise

Much research has been done into the relationship between diet, health and disease. Exercise can be as important as healthy eating. In 1799, Thomas Easton said, 'It is not the rich and the great nor those who depend on medicine who become old but such as use much exercise. For the idler never attains great age.'

It seems sensible, therefore, to take time out for exercising our bodies. This is a bit of a sore point for me. I'm not a lover of sport or walking. I do, however, love swimming, a good all-over activity for the body. Again, discipline and routine come into play; a short walk taken on a regular basis can work wonders, not just for our physical body.

A walk can be so inspiring. Nature provides us with a feast for our eyes. Maybe new friends will cross our path and remember, a stranger is a friend you have yet to meet. Once we get out and about, anything can happen, but sitting around at home procrastinating will not open any doors.

One major benefit regular physical exertion can have is to improve the function of the cardiovascular system, which in turn reduces the risk of a heart attack. Also, by burning up the energy taken from food, we can keep or reduce our body weight, depending on the amount we do. This is bound to have a strengthening effect on the body.

I once read that a lot of people are put off joining team sports because they feel they have to be perfect, always competing to win. Why cannot we just play a game for the fun, enjoying the company of team-mates? This takes the pressure off and, if we always have to be perfect at something before we can join in, most of us will never get started!

Taking Responsibility For Our Bodies

A simple routine can be a lifeline when we feel our 'get up and go' has 'got up and gone'! It may seem trifling to speak about general personal hygiene but I knew a wonderful lady, then in her eighties, who started her day off with a thorough all-over wash, not necessarily a shower or bath. She took pleasure in tending to her body and, after her wash, she would rub moisturising cream over her body. I must say at eighty she had skin that looked like a young girl's, so it had paid off!

Unfortunately, she died recently. She was a well-known artist, painter and sculptress, producing work until she died. She told me her secret was discipline, taught to her by her mother. Even as an elderly lady, she still gave thanks for what her mother had instilled in her. That stuck in my mind: discipline, routine. So simple and we can all put it into practice at any level. This training of the mind and character is designed to produce self-control and, practised often enough, becomes part of us, our way of life.

On those days when you think you have nothing to get out of bed for, the routine in itself will give you reasons to get out of bed! Once we start to love ourselves and appreciate our wonderful bodies, it becomes very gratifying to care for them.

Take our hair, for instance. When it is a mess, we feel a mess. It can make more of an impact than our clothes as we look at each other's faces when we speak and are automatically drawn to a person's hair. Try making your hairstyle a priority, instead of just a quick flick through with a comb. A new look might be just what you need. Remember, you are special, you deserve the best that life has to give you. I have found the more I reach out for life's riches, the more is made available to me.

The same principle applies when we get dressed. Let our clothes enhance our mood. Put on the best you have, that dress or trousers you were saving for a special occasion. Get it out, the time to wear it is NOW!

Life will give you another one for the next occasion. Instead of waiting for a special event, make every day a fiesta!

We should be happy to use what we have for, if we store items away instead of taking enjoyment from them, who can blame life if it thinks we don't need anything new?

Proper Food

We are what we eat. What we put into our stomachs will be digested and distributed all over our bodies and will enable us to function as efficient human beings. Over two thousand years ago Hippocrates said, 'Each one of the substances of a man's diet acts upon his body and changes it in some way and upon these changes his whole life depends, whether he be in health in sickness or convalescence.'

No Appetite

Times of stress can cause us to have virtually no appetite and then a simple diet of nutritional food is called for. The choice is enormous, so we can enjoy foods we like. It is a good idea to invest in a dietary guide book. Planning our diet, and shopping for it, will help get us motivated again. I spend hours in the library reading books about the natural medicines that can be found in the food in our larders.

Foods can have a profound effect on our mental and emotional state. Take, for instance, primitive tribes who, when they want to get into a frenzied state, drink potions of highly-charged foods or alcohol. Other cultures use the opium poppies or so-called magic mushrooms. I'm sure we have all experienced the effects of alcohol, from euphoria to black gloom. Some foods can have a relaxing effect on the body while others make us nervous and jittery.

Improved Nutrition Can Improve Our Mental State

A stronger body means a stronger mind, making it possible to do away with tranquillisers, anti-depressants and sleeping pills.

Can you believe we hold the key to our well-being? We can purchase, prepare and serve good health to ourselves with our own hands. When you are stressed or nervous, stay away or reduce your intake of refined foods, such as sugar, alcohol, tea and coffee, as they can unbalance the nervous system. Instead, give yourself plenty of fresh foods, shop around for what is in season or, better still, what comes from your own garden.

Comfort Eating

On the other hand, if you feel your appetite is on the large side, for whatever reason, don't go on a crash diet. Just love your body and in return your body will maintain its own weight and throw negative thoughts from your mind – trust that life will give you what you need.

We are fortunate today that we have more alternative therapies to help us with balancing our bodies. You will find therapists are interested in treating the whole body, not merely sticking a plaster on the spot where it hurts. Some of the more popular alternative therapies are:–

Herbalism – Herbal medicine involves the preparation of roots, leaves, stems, seeds and plants either for consumption or for use as an ointment. Herbs are available for anybody to pick and use and I have had great fun growing my own.

A good book will help with advice on these best uses or, better still, you could join a study course. If you don't have enough confidence to administer treatment yourself, get in touch with a herbalist in your area.

Aromatherapy – The term aromatherapy implies the use of our sense of smell in the prevention and treatment of disorders. However, nowadays it is most commonly used to describe a particular type of treatment in which essential oils are rubbed on the skin or used in the bath. Each kind of odour has its own particular virtue and an aromatherapy massage aids us two-fold: we get relief from the oils and a beautifully relaxing massage. Again, you can learn about it yourself or consult an aromatherapist.

Bach Flower Remedies – These consist of a number of prepared remedies derived from flowers or plants. They are named after Dr Edward Bach who said, 'Disease is in essence the result of conflict between soul and mind. So long as our soul and personalities are in harmony, all is joy, peace, happiness and health. It is when our personalities are led astray from the path laid down by the soul, whether by our own worldly desires or by the persuasion of others, that a conflict arises'.

Homeopathy – Homeopathy is a system of alternative medicine developed at the end of the eighteenth century. It is based on a belief that, when the body shows signs of illness, it is the consequence of its resistance mechanism working to repel an attack and, instead of suppressing symptoms, it may be desirable to take some form of treatment calculated to help resistance.

A little gem! The Queen's interest in homeopathy stems from childhood when her father, King George VI, used to treat both daughters this way. If you would like to try homeopathy, bear in mind a lot of preparation has gone into the remedies and it is advisable to consult those with experience in this field before attempting to treat yourself.

Anthroposophy – Rudolf Steiner, an Austrian thinker and scientist, formed his own Society in 1909. Anthroposophy was based on the Greek words anthropos, meaning man, and sophia, meaning wisdom, and stands for 'awareness'. It does not reject the tenets of orthodox medicine but insists that, instead of relying on drugs and other forms of treatment, doctors should encourage patients to look to their own lifestyles to find out why they have fallen ill. 'All healing is self-healing,' they advised. This type of medicine is much more firmly established in the rest of Europe than in Britain. Look for a practitioner in your area and ask for an appointment, but you may have to look a long way as they are few and far between.

Osteopathy – According to Dr Alan Stoddard this is, 'concerned with the establishment and maintenance of the normal structural integrity of the body.' This is done by manipulation of joints to restore them to their normal positions and mobility, giving relief to muscles and ligaments.

Osteopaths are recognised by the medical profession and its instigator, Andrew Taylor, is still himself a practising doctor. It is not difficult to find osteopaths but usually an appointment is necessary.

Massage – A technique which lies between the laying on of hands and therapeutic touch. The main aim is to promote general relaxation by relaxing muscles and removing tension, thus freeing previously contained energies.

Massage is as old as history, can be found in every culture in the world and is beneficial for mind and body alike.

'Giving massage is something everybody ought to be able to do. It isn't a mystique but a natural thing and very easy to do. I'm not talking about the hour-long professional body massage but about easing somebody's shoulders in the office or massaging your husband or wife when they get in tired from work.' Claire Maxwell Hudson, masseuse.

Again, it is not difficult to learn and can be done from a book, but the best results are obtained from a qualified masseur.

Massage should be a pleasurable experience but, when done properly, is physically taxing on the therapist. Rolfing and Shiatsu are similar in their effect.

Reflexology – The discovery by Dr W. Fitzgerald in 1920 that the body is divided into zones of energy which can be exploited for prevention and treatment is commonly known as Reflexology. By feeling patients' feet in certain prescribed ways, reflexologists can detect which energy channels are blocked. The massage may be gentle, with deep pressure applied where needed. Always seek a qualified therapist.

Acupuncture – According to Joe Goodman, ex-President of the British Acupuncture Association, this is concerned with the mental and emotional state of people and very much concerned with nutrition. It uses not only needles but also finger pressure. It uses heat, in the form of moxibustion, and nowadays laser beams and ultrasonics. Some people inject homeopathic remedies into acupuncture points. There are all sorts of ways to deal with Chi energy.

The term acupuncture comes from the Latin words acus (needle) and punctura (prick). Needles are used to puncture the skin at certain defined points in order to restore balance of Chi (energy). Consult an acupuncturist to see if this type of treatment is suitable for you; other traditional Chinese treatments might be more appropriate.

Yoga – It is based on the theory of the union of the self with higher consciousness. Gurus or instructors aim, through physical and mental exercise, to create a healthy mind in a healthy body. Yoga courses concentrate on three main aspects: posture, breathing and meditation. Classes are held in most towns.

Meditation – In India and Asia, meditation has been practised as far back as recorded history. Very simply, a mantras is used – sacred words the meditator concentrates on to rid the mind of intrusive thoughts, which dissipate energy and cause stress and suffering.

Meditation appears to be a solvent of stress. As the mind relaxes, so the body calms down too. There are many books available on the subject or you can join a class or even learn it yourself.

Reiki – The word Reiki means universal life energy and is a way of transferring this universal life energy by a hands-on healing technique based on a particular atonement process. It is a form of deep relaxation and works on the immune system, which in turn enables you to heal yourself. It is claimed to work on many different levels, both physical and mental, and all that is required of the clients is that they be open to receiving healing energy. You can find a Reiki practitioner by contacting the Association of European Reiki Practitioners.

CHAPTER 4

Down Days

Even on the uphill climb the dark clouds will still descend and the old pains of sadness and frustration will still sting the eyes.

Nobody around you wants to hear the same old story again! All you want are answers to questions, reasons why it happened at all and is still happening to you. I don't know all the answers. What can be a small hurt to one person can be a huge trauma to another.

When feelings well up, try to let them out. Cry, scream and shout. Closing the lid at these times will only cause the pressure to build up even more. Try to examine why you have these feelings and what has triggered them off. Try to turn that temporary block around and let the flowing process start again as quickly as possible. Flush those sad thoughts away. Imagine lying in a clear stream. Let the water flow over you and carry away the pain and hurt. Feel fresh new life coming over you.

If, like me, you have ever felt that whatever you try to do is not enough or important and does not make a scrap of difference to the human race, please consider this little tale from Lorans Eisley's book 'The Star Thrower'. One day he was walking along a beach where thousands of starfish had been washed up onto the shore.

He noticed a boy picking them up, one by one, and throwing them back into the ocean. When he asked him why he was doing this, the boy said, 'If I don't, they'll die!' 'But how can saving so few make any difference when so many are doomed?' the author asked. The little boy picked up another, threw it back into the ocean and said, 'It's going to make a lot of difference to this one!' Eisley was so touched he spent the rest of the day helping the boy.

That always spurs me on. Every little helps. A jigsaw is made up of many tiny pieces but just one missing piece can make a great deal of difference to the completed picture. So we are important. Our lives matter. Try saying when you feel low, 'Go on, throw another starfish back!'

If you are suffering from depression, just think, it did not come on overnight so it is not going to go overnight. Get back on the living ladder, one rung at a time, don't miss any out, and, with each step, a new lesson will be learned. Everything we learn on the way up will help to sustain us at the top. You may think it is easy for me to say it works, but I've been there, read the book, got the T-shirt. In the beginning it was hard. I doubted many times but, once I had learned to trust and not worry about the future, to take little steps of faith by trusting, not building up high hopes or thinking the worst, I found life was full of pleasant surprises.

Is There More To Life?

Do you sometimes wonder what the struggle of life is all about? Plodding on for seventy years, if we are lucky! For some, the mundane routine of life becomes a real struggle: getting up in the morning, getting food, going to work, a little play, going to bed and then start all over again. Do this for our lifetime then, puff, it's all over!

It is hard to think that one day we might be floating about like the wind. My father could always imagine himself in spirit form and he was so looking forward to what he felt was freedom, released from his material body. He often joked about the time when he would look down at those still on earth. He pictured himself laughing as he floated around, so happy to be free.

When we experience what we think to be a good day, life is very sweet. With perfect health and youth on our side, I can imagine no better place to be than on earth. There is so much to see. I would love to be able to travel to the four corners of the globe. To see all that grows and moves without having to worry about a thing. I feel we are so wonderfully made that there has to be more than just this lifetime. What, where or when I cannot say, but I intend to live this life with that in mind.

Q. Why does our mind go into a depressed state ?
A. The mind is both strong and weak and many people allow wrong thinking. Thinking alters our decisions. Power-pack the thinking part of the brain and it will become a strong tool.

Strength is the secret weapon when it comes to depression. A flower, starved of the right conditions, becomes frail. It is the same with human beings. The conditions we surround ourselves with are so important for, once the body is weakened, the mind follows. Take away something of great joy in our lives and it weakens us. Busy people, those with a purpose, never get the kind of depression that debilitates. Instead of keeping depressed souls quiet on calming pills, a very strict programme of activity has a much more rewarding result.

The more information we store in the brain, the better we are able to withstand hard knocks. Instantly, a plan of action springs to mind. Maybe another experience can be of help; if we have been alert enough to see another's pain, the way they dealt with it comes back in a flash. Alert is a good word, don't you think? Perhaps, over the years, those who are regarded as nosy are not far off the mark. They are the ones who observe a change in circumstances and are wide awake to what goes on around them. Many a nosy neighbour has saved a situation.

Build up knowledge. Start with the things you like best for, if a spark is already in you, the fire will burn quicker. Never be afraid to voice a question. It is by asking that we start the communication process, an ever opening process. Depression closes our mind, hence the need to be active as quickly as possible.

If you feel a depressed state coming on, take action. Join a club, enrol in a course at your local school or college and ram your head full of knowledge. Don't delay, don't sit and confirm your feelings. Feed the body and mind with new ideas and you will find there is no time to feel down. There's too much going on. Time on our hands needs to be put to good use and there are so many avenues open to us. If finances are not a priority, voluntary work is very fulfilling. Find out what is available in your area. What would you enjoy the best? Very few turn volunteers away – an extra pair of hands is always gratefully received. So the mind is sustained and, instead of crying like a baby, we will roar like a lion!

Q. What is the power behind suicide ?

A. Take a person with a broken heart: the bleeding process has already started, life energies have started to flow out and the lack of understanding prevents reliance on greater forces than oneself.

Suicide is the ultimate negative energy. We are created to live forever, and only extreme conditions would cause us to forget this. Very often such deaths are blamed on failure but I say to you it is lack of love for, if it was only failure, the suicide rate would be enormous.

I cannot emphasise the importance of love. Drop everything in your life in order to find it or give it, as there is no greater preventative medicine or cure available. There are those who are loved greatly but, because they put up a barrier of negativity, they prevent the love getting through. These are the saddest cases of all, for surely love should be able to break down such barriers. A long-standing hurt regarding love is greater than the love being given. The person concerned has never been able to release that hurt and it remains like a stone. Only a greater love can force that away and sometimes a simple act can turn stone back into flesh, such as the birth of a baby. This can be so powerful that many a stony heart has melted by the simple joy and, touched by new life, an out-pouring of love will save that person. Even those with serious health conditions will fight to stay alive if a birth is imminent.

Are you causing negativity to another human being? If so, stop right now. If you no longer feel you can give love, for goodness sake, don't give out the opposite. Remove yourself rather than directly cause pain and make space for love to find a way. Doing things for the wrong reasons will only cause disaster.

Heaping negative vibes continuously on a person is as dangerous as severing a main artery. Be aware of thought, word and action. You can lift others, even be responsible for breaking through a negative barrier, and thus preventing suicide.

Q. How can suicidal feelings be reversed?
A. A reverse gear needs to be found, but this is not easy to do. Suicidal thinking needs to be halted, as thought may be expressed in words and actions and, by controlling your thoughts, you are able to allow only positive ones to be expressed.

You need to go into hard training for such an important step. Instead of condemning yourself, start to see the beauty which exists in the human body and appreciate how each part works. Even if you don't like the shape of, say, your legs, if they enable you to walk each day they are performing the task for which they were designed. So, instead of finding fault, look for the good points and in the end you will feel ashamed that you even considered destroying such a wonderful machine.

However, do not put your trust in your own strength alone, but lean on higher, spiritual forces. A desire to die is a wish for your present circumstances to end, not you as a person. Reach out for a rebirth, start learning new ideals and let the old you be dead and buried, in a figurative sense. Stick with the old body, for in the past it has been abused by the fuel of the mind, and start to treat it with love. Look only to what gives a warm feeling. Wrap yourself in a blanket of warming love. The future holds new and exciting reasons to stay alive. Give yourself one last chance to find out how true this is. Look for the light. All living cells function on a higher level when exposed to light, not just the literal light which comes from the sun, but light-hearted attitudes, wanting to be seen with nothing to hide. Find those who work for light and be part of the greater power source needed to bring light to others in dark places. Great suffering makes great people. Quickly turn your life around, to drive with a new-found power into the future. You can and will succeed !

Q. How should family react towards those who are depressed ?
A. Family members should act as a tower of strength.

> 'Life is not all froth and bubble,
> Two things stand alone,
> Friendship in another's trouble
> Courage in your own.'

For you never know when trouble will knock at your door. If you need a friend you should first learn to be one. Open your arms, be the first to give a cuddle and ask questions later.

Family reassurance is so important. We make jokes about being able to pick friends but not family, but genuine family care need never leave members feeling this way. Yes, it is understandable when negative attitudes come from families, and this can drive a wedge, but once we start to be aware of what we give out, a warmer relationship will form with everyone. Perhaps you are already a loving individual and do not need to ask what to do, because you are already too busy doing it.

For those who have had no experience in dealing with depression, just simply be there for that person. It is not always necessary actually to do anything for them. When we just sit quietly, it is amazing what passes between two people. On the other hand, some would rather be more practical and this can be important as the everyday mundane tasks can seem impossible when life becomes 'a space between two books'. I cannot emphasise the importance of love and, even when you feel like screaming, just count to ten and, little by little, the situation will improve. Try to understand the sick person, give thanks that you are able to be there for them. Touch can be like a magic spell – see the joy when we extend a hand or embrace. Do it with real meaning and send love to your family. You can walk through fire if clothed in love.

Q. How can we add colour and style to our lives ?
A. Colour is as individual as a fingerprint. Start taking notice of the patterns in all that surrounds you and bring nature into your home. Collect leaves, shells and feathers, in fact, anything that inspires you. Collect unusual items on holiday, give them a special place in your home and you will find you re-live the holiday through these items.

Style is your particular way of putting your taste together and nobody can take that uniqueness away from you. Start to bring out the very essence of yourself, be your own judge, stand by what pleases you and you will find that, as your confidence grows, your individual style will shine forth.

Don't let anyone smother your character, for every hue of every part of life makes the wonderful variety of colour, literally and figuratively. Headings like right and wrong are so narrow, the gap between is enormous. Much nicer to see each other as 'different' as it stops the judging process. Stamp out an emblem for yourself !

Love

When you get up in the morning, dress yourself with love from the tip of your head to the tip of your toes.

Be determined to be a loving person today. Simple acts of love are based on true love for others. Appreciate even the smallest areas of daily living. See love as a giant ball of gold, touching everything you do with a dusting of gold. No qualification is needed before we practise love. The more we do it the easier it becomes. As has been said before, it is one thing we can give away that yet remains with us. Something so powerful cannot be manufactured. There are many commercial products made to encourage us to show love. In fact, we have all we need right within our very being.

Let the world see your heart and don't be afraid of rejection as love will conquer all in the end. The giving of our love is the all important thing. Doors of steel will melt away if opened with keys of love. The smallest act will be recognised as equal to the greatest. For how can we judge what is great or small. A small gesture, when greatly needed, is truly magnificent to that person.

Be brave enough to give it a go. Don't let cynicism hold you back. Excuses will spring to mind but learn to rid your mind of these. Soon they will give up and only loving gestures will break through. In the end love becomes a way of life.

Partner

When you come home from a busy day at work, do you snap at the person you chose to share your most intimate moments with or do you greet that person with open arms, desperate to be home in their presence after hours of separation? Forget the daily tasks for five minutes. See only this beloved person. Really look at your partner, touch each other and genuinely ask what sort of day they have had.

Take time to connect with the space around you. The day has filled it with all sorts of things. Now you are with your other half, so let that show. How wonderful a day can be when love touches it.

Make yourself approachable. Your partner will confide in you, feel happy to release a problem, knowing you will listen and find a solution, using love to smooth any rough edges.

All too often we hear, 'Oh don't bother me now, I'm tired.' Calm yourself down. Look happy on seeing your loved one. If both partners know this will be the greeting, all tiredness will be instantly gone. In fact, the heart will be glad to return to the place it wants to be more than anywhere else in the world.

Once home, stop everything for a few minutes. What is so desperate? The post? A hot drink? Instead give a loving greeting. It will do you far more good!

Being Considerate

Delays can be distressing if you are waiting for someone. If for any reason you are likely to be delayed, try to dispel fears by getting word to your partner. A few minutes forethought can save a lot of unnecessary heartache.

Just ask yourself, what would a loving person do, and go ahead and do it. If you are a family person, this atmosphere will soon rub off on children. They will know what to expect on entering home. This is the place where love greets them at the door!

A mild answer turns away wrath and a kiss and a cuddle will go down a whole lot better than a grunt!

Be aware of the present atmosphere in your home. Do you feel good about it? If not, why? What can be done to make it more loving?

Is it just a surface alteration or are deep questions called for? Our needs and wants get a bit mixed up. Try making a list of priorities. It can come as quite a shock how little we need!

Sometimes deep emotions are kept well hidden, emotions about love. Let those around you know, by bringing down your defences. This will cause others to want to do the same. The hustle and bustle of everyday life clouds a lot of good intentions. In the end we don't bother. We shelve things or bottle them up.

When the opportunity does present itself we let it go, a beautiful moment lost. Catch these moments from now on, sprinkle them with that wonderful golden dust, and love will do the rest!

At Work

Are you dreaded at work? Do members of staff avoid you whenever possible? Are you like a bear with a sore head as soon as you step inside the work place? It might not be the place you most want to be right now, but for obvious reasons you have to be. Give thanks for yourself, for your ability to do the work, then reach out to others who may also be feeling the way you do. How can you contribute to making this part of your daily life more pleasant? Try bringing a bit of love to work today!

At School

If your day starts with a bus journey, be aware of your manners on the bus. Be an example of how to be orderly. Give a cheery greeting to fellow school mates. Show respect to the teachers - after all they are your source of tuition. Soak up the information given. Remember, a little praise and thanks goes a long way. Speak truthfully and act honestly. Dishonest acts are so difficult to turn around. Far better to keep a clean slate!

Before loosing your 'cool' at school, think twice!

While Shopping

Be courteous with shop assistants. A little smile will cheer the day along! Complaints can be put over in a mild form. Stay calm and give others the chance to correct any errors.

The old saying 'you catch more flies with sugar than vinegar' applies in all situations. Shopping trips will become joyous occasions, leaving us eager to return home to enjoy our purchases!

To love is to forgive all, no matter what. Everybody needs to feel loved. If any message is to be given it is this: LOVE DISPELS ANGER!

What funny creatures we are. If we can't have our own way anger so easily comes to the surface. Why is it so hard see another person's point of view or just to accept?

Love The Garden

My small garden, which was planted with cuttings given from friends and family, now resembles a mini jungle. I took such pleasure in the planting and tending. The more love I poured on them the more they grew.

I get so much enjoyment just from looking at the array of colours. I am so thankful for my little garden. If plants respond like this, how much more fulfilling it is to shower people with love, to mix the right actions with words, to cultivate a world of beautiful people, as different from one another as the flowers in my garden. Love doesn't mean cloning.

Because I disturb the soil on a regular basis, I hardly ever get weeds taking a firm hold. Again this can apply to life. If we disturb the nasty attitudes, allowing only positive thinking to root firmly, life's garden will be exquisite.

I like this poem by Ella Wheeler Wilcox.

As you go through life

Don't look for the flaws as you go through your life;
And even when you find them, It is wise and kind to be somewhat blind.

And look for the virtue behind them,
For the cloudiest night has a hint of light
Somewhere in its shadows hiding,

It is better by far to hunt for a star
Than the spots on the sun abiding.

The current of life runs ever away
To the bosom of God's great ocean,
Don't set your force against the river's course
And think to alter its motion
Don't waste a curse on the universe –
Remember it lived before you.
Don't butt at the storm with your puny form,
But bend and let it go o'er you.

The world will never adjust itself
To suit your whims to the letter.
Some things must go wrong your whole life long,
and the sooner you know it the better.
It is folly to fight with the infinite,
And go under at best in the wrestle:
The wiser man shapes into God's plan
As water shapes into a vessel.

Take Time Out for Yourself

Do you fell guilty about taking time off to enjoy yourself?

Busy people often feel like getting away then chastise themselves. They look for company to share the time with, giving to others instead of themselves.

Sometimes it does one good to take a few hours out, purely for oneself. Take a walk, go somewhere quiet, read a book, pamper yourself with a beauty treatment or a relaxing massage. Enjoy one of the many alternative therapies now available, like aromatherapy or reflexology. Take a camera to a favourite spot and capture the sight on film. Only afterwards will the benefits hit home. If, like me, you have neglected such things, I know the joy will be tremendous.

We all need to recharge our batteries from time to time. The first time I experienced a professional massage I couldn't believe how relaxed I felt. I slept for hours afterwards (thanks, Jennifer).

We can always find an excuse not to spoil ourselves. It is wise to set a few hours aside and be determined to make this 'your time'.

During this time forget the everyday problems and give yourself over completely to whatever you have decided to do. When you think of the hours we give to other pursuits - working, caring for the family, helping parents or relatives, etc, a few hours now and again is not unreasonable!

I'm sure many do this as a matter of course but those of us who have neglected this, for whatever reason, can now make a consciouse decision to change.

I often treat myself to favourite foods, items not enjoyed by the rest of the family. I love dried dates and figs, also Turkish Delight - YUM. We all have specialities that tickle our taste buds, but we often go without these treats because of family budgets, not wanting to be selfish. Careful budgeting will allow for a few of these luxuries.

Advice On How to Go Forward

Walking forward involves putting one step in front of another. Likewise, one needs to expand the thinking process, and seek new ground. Remember, to stand still is to fall behind. To win a race, one first has to enter and run! Pick up the ideas sent out by others, be alert to see gaps in whatever enters your space. Build small castles. Every mark we make remains. Every house has many bricks and the individual bricks are as important as the mass. Stretch out your hand. Be ready to receive. Those not expecting to get anything mostly get their wish. Pick up the ball and run forward, it's the only way to score a goal. Be a player not a spectator.

Mind Power

Many people have become trapped in a totally materialistic way of thinking. Of course we all love material belongings, but our desire for them is upside down. Everything we need will be given on a plate, once we harness our thoughts. Simple is indeed beautiful. The path to our heart's desires is as easy as falling asleep in an armchair.

Most people will lack the trust to try such a method. Those already practising this incredible way of life will not have any doubts. Very successful people have discovered this process by trial and error or have been introduced to it by a fellow believer. The only way to test this method is to give it a go. It doesn't cost a penny! How many schemes have you already been offered and at what price? I don't have to sit up at night twidling my thumbs, wondering what will be. I decide what I want, programme it into my mind and then enjoy a well deserved rest from a successful day's activity.

In order for the mind to make plans come into fruition, our conscious mind needs to withdraw. That is why meditation works. Instead of running around like a headless chicken trying to bring things about, first stop and try to imagine what it is you want, and ask yourself, do you really want this? Half the time we want what other people make us believe we want, what we cannot live without. Pick up any paper or magazine, switch on the television and listen to the advertisements. This is programming our minds. I encourage you to go one better and programme your own mind, set up your own channel, learn how to switch it on before you go to sleep. I do this all the time with amazing results.

Did you know that the most influential men and women do this all the time? This is a two-way enterprise: once you know and ask for a particular set of events to happen, you have to take the staring role. After all, this is what you have asked for. Once you allow doubt to enter, the process is halted. You are causing this, so be aware of your thoughts after you start to practise this method. Doubt and fear have such devastating effects on the body. I like the example of walking the plank: place a plank on the ground and most people would walk it without thinking twice. Raise that same plank off the ground and suddenly doubt and fear creeps in; maybe I will fall! What was an easy task becomes more difficult. If we do away with doubt and fear and tell ourselves, of course we can do it, then we will.

Visualization

It takes a lot of practise to perfect this, just like everything in life that is worthwhile. The rewards will astound you, inspiring you to make this visualization a way of life for ever.

When I lay in my bed I first say my prayers and thank God for the wonderful day, then I switch on my mind channel. I firstly play previous programmes not yet realised in the material world. It becomes cosy returning to areas I now accept as mine. Then I design new programmes. Sometimes they are very simple and very easy to visualise. The colours come vivid and fast. Other things can take longer to form, and we will need to return to this night after night until they are exactly what we want. For example, I know my next car, I see the model, the colour, I get in and drive it, I even take my family with me, and it becomes part of other plans I make. I take it from one programme to another. It becomes so easy and such fun. At first I had a problem with the colour – how did I solve this? Why, by visiting a garage that sold my car. I looked hard and long at the colour. After that it was easy! That, by the way, is an excellent way of finding out what you really would like, be it cars, property, clothes, in fact anything. If you cannot personally check something out, see if a book exists relating to your desire. If not you will just have to invent it or call on a team of experts to do that for you. All is possible when you are the director.

Are you getting the picture? More importantly, do you like it? Of course, not everyone will like this method, which is why so many people do not get out of life any more than they have at this moment of reading. They may be quite satisfied with their way of life - that is fine by me. All I know is that life has been so exciting and easy for me since I became aware of the power of the mind. My life is never dull. I never have to be anxious any more. All I have to do is think about what I would like to do next. It is wonderful, a bit like day dreaming, but this time I can dream knowing that if I truly desire something I can put it in my nightly programme.

When we sit down and work out what will bring us lasting joy, it is surprising how simple that turns out to be. Very often we have let our lives get a little out of control. Before we know it we are on this treadmill and we have to keep going for fear that if we stop our whole world will fall apart. We find we are involved in jobs, committees, all sorts of things we increasingly find we hate.

Direct your mind to get you out. Try to see the ideal situation for yourself. It doesn't happen overnight. I have known people who, for whatever reasons, cannot stand their present situation and, within hours, change course, no matter what it costs, preferring to stop than go on. We can all make changes if we really want to. This method I use greatly helps. Somehow it stamps what we want on a great noticeboard, advertising for a new start, and it happens! I could sit all day puzzling how on earth this works. I trust visualisation because I have witnessed the results. The more energy I give to my nightly programmes, the more powerful it is. I can only tell what is working for me and ask you to try it for yourself.

This is one small example: I saw myself sitting at a desk in my home. At the time I could not afford to buy a desk, but I cleared an area ready for it. A friend called, I told her what the space was for and straight away she offered a desk that she was no longer using. Soon funds became available for me to buy one and my friend was able to sell her desk. It was a perfect arrangement at that time! This is just one of many experiences I have had.

As long as our wants are not rooted in greed and a selfish demonstration of power over another, this method will open up a new way of looking at the world, and maybe even end some of the selfishness of man. When we trust we will be given all we need, we will no longer want what another has. We only have to concern ourself with what we need. Wonderful, isn't it!

Life is very strange. Sometimes, just when we think we have it cracked, hey presto! another spanner is thrown into the works. I believe this is life's way of making us look at our possibilities. Once I started to connect situations, patterns formed. I stopped shooting about aimlessly and now I rely on my intelligence a lot more. I still love spontaneity and I find the more I think constructively, the more beautiful my natural feelings are.

By allowing people to gain their own experiences, which might involve non-judgemental input from us, we stop feeling hurt if they do not act on our advice. There is no need to harbour disapproving thoughts, which might lead to unkind words. Let us free our minds from all this unnecessary weight, for that is what it feels like. Haven't you ever rid yourself of angry thoughts, only to feel a big weight has lifted, leaving this light happy feeling?

By constantly guarding our thoughts we can save a lot of heartache. Usually those closest to us get the worst when we are angry, over, say, a domestic situation. We can quickly forget these are the folk who love us the most. If we only reminded ourselves of this point before we started shouting. Would a loved one purposely do anything to hurt or harm us?

Are other factors involved? Always try to get a full picture before flying off the handle. Try to come from a loving angle rather than prejudging the situation. If we did this, having to say sorry would be a thing of the past. Maybe that is what is meant by 'loving someone is never having to say sorry.' We would do away with wretched scenes.

Children would benefit from this too. When we come across a situation where we feel a child has done wrong or made a mistake, very often we are governed by anger, condemning before we have fully understood the situation. I know in the past I have been guilty of this, later regretting my anger. More often than not, children are unaware of consequences when they set out on a particular path. Loving parental guidance will remove fear from a child's mind, the fear of always being told off when they do something wrong. Otherwise they grow up unsure of reaching out for what life has on offer, afraid they will be chastised rather than understood.

Talking – teaching children the 'thinking first' process, and how this will guide our actions, will put them on an incredibly privileged path, demonstrating the idea that all is possible, with no boundaries to fence them in. They are unique, seeking the way that will bring them whatever they find their particular perfection to be.

I do believe we are all capable of performing one act to perfection. The only trouble is we are conditioned to look for a lifestyle that the media approves of. By talking with our children from an early age about this wonderful individual that lives inside each and every one of us, we nurture a seed that will flourish into a magnificent human being.

If we see a world with plenty, enough to go around, we are always rich, no matter what our bank balance might or might not show! We do not need to be means tested before we can practise love. As soon as we give one heartful out it replenishes itself immediately asking nothing in return. Love is the solution and the reward.

I remember reading in my mother's Autograph book, 'many are

called but few get up.' The call goes out to all those who feel unfulfilled - now is the time to appreciate the power of our own minds. Pause for thought! Harness your mind and guide your thoughts on an inward search to find your kernel. A dot is all it takes to start the outward spiral. The smallest desire can be the key to unlock the door to a more fulfilling life. I've heard it said more than once that time appears to stand still when we are doing what we love, so engrossed are we, one hundred per cent concentrated on that activity.

The speed at which we become skilled, doing what we enjoy, outweighs the struggle of doing what we hate.

I see it in my sons. They soon became experts at what they enjoyed doing. Once they were brave enough to drop things which did not fulfil them, they have never looked back.

We must wake up to the fact that we all have choices and do away with cliches like 'that's just me' or 'I can't help it.' The secret is knowing we are in control of those choices. Practise this to prove it to yourself.

A drunk has the choice to drink or refrain from alcohol. We must make the choice before we can bring it about. Before I became pregnant, I was scared of giving birth. I longed for a child, and yet I was frightened. Once I looked around me and saw just how many babies are born every day, I thought to myself, well it can't be that bad. Once I had removed the fear, by putting that reassuring thought in place, I never gave it another thought and went on to give birth to three fine sons.

What do we come back to every time - the mind!

I have always been fascinated by the reasons people do or do not do certain things. Experience will make two people faced with the same situation act differently. Once we go though an experience we are prepared for the choice we would make a second time around.

It is wonderful to think we have this freewill to make choices. I am more respectful of other people's decisions now I understand that it is up to me to make my decisions. I am responsible for the steps I take. If asked, we can lovingly share our experiences with others, but at the end of the day they must decide for themselves.

With regard to my own children I have always tried to give them roots and wings. This might sound contradictory, but when we understand the power of the mind, this is perfect. The root source of our mind needs to be developed, enabling us to be fed wherever our journey leads us.

The origin of all remains inside of our own body and mind. Armed with this thought we are equiped to make our lives spectacular. My belief that we are complete for our time on this earth stems back to what I was taught as a little girl, namely that we are made in God's image, that we have Godly attributes - we cannot fail!

Believe everything is possible for the way we want to live and it will be. That means don't wish for another's dream, only be concerned with your own. If you are a plum why try to be a banana? Accept the wonderful creation that you are and highlight your unique qualities.

How often have we heard it said, 'He's a natural.' We are all naturals once we discover and pursue our own talents.

Mind power has always been known, as in sayings like 'mind over matter'. Somehow this has been over-shadowed by clever business people using advertising to brainwash us into their way of thinking. Even children are more inclined to be sheep: must have designer labels and the latest of everything. Yet when I read background information about successful writers they have mostly had an out-of-the-ordinary upbringing. Some parents have chosen to 'opt' out of the run-of-the-mill society, living like nomads, making their children stand out from the designer-label kids. All of this built character within those kids which comes across very strongly in their writing.

If we can get across this message of individualism to young people, I'm sure they would find life more exciting.

I always fought hard for my children to be themselves, to be bold enough to stand out in a crowd. What you believe in is what makes you the special person you are.

I feel strongly about the way we behave with children and young people. Those tender shoots can so easily be damaged. How rewarding it is to encourage strong growth, to support their individualism. Teach them never to climb to the top by standing on another person, but rather to walk side by side with respect.

Power doesn't lie just in the physical body – just look at the number of physically handicapped people who achieve through intelligence and determination. Accident victims who have been told they will never walk again, by programming their mind to accept the opposite, have walked and carried on with careers. If you have never been fully aware of what can be achieved by mind over matter, give it a go. We can all decide to help ourselves, no matter what level we start at.

For me, it even helps to get the housework done quickly and efficiently. I just visualise my jobs beforehand, see the speed with which I will perform them and it happens. I am so pleased to have completed them so well, I never see any job as distasteful, only necessary.

I give the example of housework because most people find it a boring chore, one to be got out of the way quickly. To keep house properly can be turned into an art or business. Concentrate on performing every aspect methodically, creating a beautiful home environment, not just a place to lay your head.

I believe we all have a mission to achieve. Maybe getting these words in print is mine, and maybe these words were written just for you, helping you to pick up your ball and run with it. I certainly hope so. Take heart if you are feeling trapped – **now** is the time to plan your great escape. I read about a man who was locked up in a prison of war camp. He visualised getting out, he programmed his mind every night, saw himself walking in a beautiful town, and driving in his car. It became real to him. One day the guard mistook the number of men who were sent out of the camp for manual labour. The man hung back after the day's work and was able to slip away. No one noticed until the next day, giving him time to get away. Eventually he fulfilled his vision and walked into that town.

When circumstances present a solution to a desire, we need to be ready to act, just like the prisoner. We need to learn to trust. After a few experiences of this working, it becomes easier to believe it will work.

Shell-Shock

Being positive and focused on what we want out of life does not immune us from the occasional bombshell. When this happens we need time to get over the initial blow. It can and does hit one for six. My first reaction when I was suffering was to throw all I had learnt straight out through the door. Circumstances not going as we would like can cause this automatic self-defence mechanism to lash out.

Gradually I have come to understand this feeling. I now let the shell-shock subside. I try to switch off from circumstances for at least a day. I get out of the house, keep away from any one who is likely to want to talk about the trouble. I find my emotions calm down, so I can clear my thinking, see the overall picture of life and get things into perspective. By stepping away from a situation we can sometimes see it quite differently. Once I feel in control of myself again, it is easier to pick up the pieces, examine the facts and see how they relate to me. I can evaluate what can be saved or gained, who needs help, sympathy, whatever. I am much more able to find the energy to help when I am calm. Being upset and angry just saps me of my strength. Finally I come back on course, only to find my positive attitude is still intact. I'm once again ready to go. Sometimes it takes a little longer than others, but so far it has not failed to return.

I would still prefer to see the glass half full than half empty. It has always helped me to talk to people with similar experiences, especially those who have survived. It gives me ideas to focus on and programme into my mind. People who are enthusiastic, and passionate about a particular subject, can give one such a boost, that little bit of encouragement needed to spur us on when we are still recovering from shell-shock. It goes without saying that we need to give this help when the tables are turned.

The other day I met a lady who told me that she had made a promise to herself – because she had received help, she would help somebody, or try to do some good, every day. She has never stopped giving thanks for the help she recieved. Her kindness to others resulted in many gifts for her garden. Do you know I have never seen a garden flourish like hers, a true example of what you give out you get back.

Life

What is this life all about? How many times have we asked that question? Well, what is the answer? Life, I'm afraid, is what we make it, by being positive in our attitude and keeping our mind firmly on what we want out of life. For instance, I am trying to keep free from unnecessary stress, so I put aside any problems that do not directly concern me. I do not have to be cold towards another's trouble. I can give my loving support but still distance myself, so as not to upset my emotional balance.

I have decided to deal with my worries as quickly as possible. Any unpleasant business has to be dissected, sorted and put to rest, allowing my mind to be at peace. From experience, I know only to well what pain nervous tension can cause. The physical symptoms are very real. It is as though my body has a fever. My stomach feels sick. I know this is triggered by the worry passing through my mind. The sooner I replace those thoughts with calming, positive ones, the sooner the physical symptoms depart.

I do believe that as we get older we are more able to do this. We have learnt the futility of needless worry. I now appreciate how precious time is. I want to fill it with constructive behaviour. Even sitting resting has to be productive. I do not want to sit with a head full of problems, so when I sit I condition myself not to fuss about anything. What I haven't dealt with on that day will have to wait until the 'morrow. More and more I am practicing a 'switch off' routine, and by doing this I reserve my energies. Jobs that are left are just the same when I do address them. Very few get more difficult. In fact I approach them with greater vigour, having recharged my batteries. By confronting and dealing with the troubles that invade our space on a daily basis, we are better able to keep up in this race called life.

For years I felt I was running in sixth place. I could see the ones out in front but I could never catch up. Once I started to see only myself in the race, I was always the winner. I am the winner!

PART 2

CHAPTER 5

Self

Self! One's own person or individuality!

Who are we? Have you ever asked that question? How would we describe ourselves? It might seem a funny thing to ask but why not? We are so used to seeing other people's characters, their likes and dislikes.

When one of my sons walks into a room, the expression on his face usually gives me a clue as to the kind of day he is having. Are we aware of our expressions? Do we sometimes overreact to certain situations? Why not analyse these patterns and try to understand just who this person is that we walk around with every day?

How often do we change ourselves to fit in with family or friends? We change our ideas to suit those around us. Understandably, we do this out of kindness and consideration but, at the same time, we are not being true to ourselves and, in the end, we absorb all these different views.

Life goes on at such a pace that we end up not knowing what we really feel. Sometimes I long to wash off the vibes of others in order to find my own thoughts.

Think of the food you serve when you have family or friends to stay. Eager to please, you try to cook what they like and the normal routine goes haywire. Then, when they return home, you make your favourite dish just the way you like it, and you sigh with pleasure.

We should lead our lives the way we feel happiest and not let other people upset our good feeling. Cast off anger that was picked up from another. Just because your neighbour is in a bad temper does not mean you have to be. Let us be bold in showing our individuality. Let us not be overly concerned with the comings and goings of others. This is a time to get the balance back in our lives.

We are all on different levels of learning and understanding. Once we accept this, it should stop us from getting upset about things we do not understand or, once we do understand, from becoming impatient with others not yet there. An elderly Dutch lady once said to me, 'The thief must steal and murderer must murder. Do not be anxious about these things.'

Yes, we should show compassion and send our prayers to help the victims and criminals. Just like the ripples on a pool our thoughts spread far, for good or bad. When we are in a bad mood, it so easily rubs off on the whole household. Likewise, happiness is infectious.

When I have to confront someone about a problem, I am careful to do it calmly, allowing time for them to speak their feelings. But not when they are about to embark on a car journey, in case what I have said affects their concentration.

What stuff are we made of? What is our character? Do we like what we see? If not, why? Can we be more balanced, likeable people? We have to live with ourselves for a very long time. Let us enjoy our own company and be true to what is in our own hearts.

Mostly, illness comes when we go against the grain. Maybe the time is now to say, 'I stop this way of life.' Again, once we let go, we make space for the new. Maybe, in this case, the new will really be the old you, the you that has been lost on the way.

Like an overgrown garden, we become tangled in the weeds and creepers. They cover and strangle the beauty that lies beneath. Be ruthless, cut the ties that bind and get order back into your life. Let sunshine and light into your heart and let your full beauty be seen.

One day, like Susan Jeffers, we will utter this prayer:

Prayer of Gratitude and Trust

I trust that no matter what happens in my life,
It is for my highest good.
And no matter what happens in the
lives of those I love,
It is for their highest good.

From all things that are put before us, we shall become stronger and
more loving people.
I am grateful for all the beauty and opportunity
you put into my life.
And in all that I do, I shall seek to be a
channel for your love.
Thank You

Personal Imprint

Personal imprint – the way we do things, our conduct, the choice of what we live with. All strong imprints of us!

You will find the time will come when you will feel better, not quite ready to take on the world and his wife, but well enough to want to make an impression again.

The minute I step out of bed, I'm ready to go, go! I like to have a routine in the morning. I like to face the day washed, dressed and make-up on; I keep my cosmetics well organised. I like my dressing table to be well lit and beautiful items to hand, such as a silver brush and hand mirror set, given to me many years ago by my husband. A well-designed wardrobe enables easy access to clothes and shoes. I hate hassle when selecting which clothes to wear. I like to know what goes with what and where it is. I keep a small box with antiseptic creams and lotions, Raljax for aches and pains, Vic for the chest!

Out of choice, I like a warm bedroom. I'm not one for a cool room with a gale blowing through the window! I keep a little radio handy – you never know when you will feel like a little soft music. I like an alarm clock near, ready for those early mornings. If I never have tea in bed, it wouldn't bother me, as I like to get up once I'm awake – no time to sit and sip tea.

I have strong feelings about the type of china I use; I have a weakness for beautiful thin china and my pet hate is tea from a mug. It wouldn't be so bad if they came with saucers, somewhere to put your teaspoon.

I like my tea made in a teapot with the milk put into the cup first. I like brown sugar served with coffee and white with tea. A clean tablecloth makes all the difference to a well laid table. I tend to eat by the clock rather than when I'm hungry.

I love beautiful writing paper and an ink fountain pen. My home is full of books so, if I need information, I have it to hand. I like to read about other people's experiences, what makes them tick. In the past, I've had a tendency to hoard old things. Now, if I have to part with something, it no longer troubles me. I'm a people's person. Material possessions are losing their importance as I get older. The deeper, meaningful human values are what I'm searching for. Maybe the depression I went through triggered off the search for a deeper meaning to life. Through the words of others, I know I am not alone in this. Sometimes I write down my thoughts only to have them confirmed by another writer. It is good to talk with like-minded folk, nice to know you are on a par with others who want more out of life than three square meals a day.

I still have a few treasures which were left to me by my family. I like to tell the history of these to my sons, not knowing if they will have the same appreciation one day. I remember seeing a film, a bit far-fetched, of a mother who died, then a year later, with a witch's spell, was brought back to life (everything is possible in films!). She walked into her son's home, now a married man, and on his kitchen window sill stood her herb pots with freshly growing herbs. She had loved and carefully tended these herb pots and was so touched to think her son had kept a part of what she loved with him. We never know what will stand out after we are gone, a small keepsake can bring back memories of a loved one. I wonder if this book will be that for my sons!

It can be fun to take a look at your personal imprint instead of thinking you are one of the crowd. You will find you are very much an individual with a 'tic' of your own.

Take a few minutes to write down your likes and dislikes.

CHAPTER 6

Taking Action

A re you enjoying life or are you stagnating?
A simple example taken from the Bible helped me:
'Ask and it shall be given to you: seek and ye shall find: knock and it shall be opened unto you. For everyone that asketh, receiveth: and he that seeketh, findeth: and to him that knocketh, it shall be opened.'

Is there something that you dream about achieving? Well, dream no more. Listen to the profound words of Matthew. Perhaps you think it sounds too simple but the one way to find out is to put it into practice. Try asking for help from a higher source than yourself. If you have never believed in such a power, maybe now is a good time to start. **The proof of the pudding is in the eating.**

If we are given advice by someone who has experienced the benefits of such advice, it can do us no harm to give it a try. Look at what we are told: 'ask and it shall be given.' Very positive indeed. How often do we hesitate to ask a friend for help, thinking we will be turned away. If only we had more trust in our fellow man. It is by asking that we make people aware of what we need. So too with universal power, or God's power. If we can learn to ask, very soon the great invisible network will pick it up thus searching for the means to bring our needs about.

Secondly, we need to seek in order to find. Open your eyes and your mind. Search for the opportunities to bring your dreams to fruition. If your dream is to ride a horse, it's no use sitting at home watching television. Put yourself in the horse world. If you have always wanted to play a musical instrument, what is stopping you? Search for that music store, delay no longer.

So Ask and Seek

Finally, knock at that door. Don't stand looking at it. We can only find out what is on the other side by making it known we are requesting the door to be opened. If we trust that God will help, he will. I have a friend who always says, 'If God doesn't come, he sends.' She is still enjoying life at the ripe old age of eighty-five. I implore you to practise this daily. I do it all the time and it works for me.

Are you feeling depressed? Do you feel as if the joy of life is passing you by?

Now is the time to ask. You need the joy of life to flow through you like fresh spring water. Stagnant water remains stagnant, free flowing water brings new energy with it. How can we start this process flowing in us? By giving, we will receive. Doing a kind deed to another by giving something away, allows new things to come to us. What can we give? Almost anything – time, money, love. Everyone of us needs something so it should not be difficult to find a needy person, but by needy I do not necessarily mean poor.

Think of the old apple tree. When the fruit falls, it is there for all who sit beneath it. Our needs differ – some are desperate materially, others are hungry for love. Once we give, be it ever so humble, we will be rewarded. Again, practise this and you will find it is true.

Cast your bread on the waters and it shall be returned a hundred-fold

The law - as we give so shall we receive - can be enforced when we start a new life. What we have done to others, we will have done to us. Give out love and happiness and love will flow into our lives. If you have come to a turning point in your life, please try these simple things. By asking and giving and loving, we are allowing the universal energy to flow freely. Not only will your standard of life improve, but your general well-being will shine and others will want to know your secret.

Here's an example of a lady asking for help. While at a coffee shop the other week, I happened to meet a lovely lady. We chatted, as ladies do, and she told me how she desperately needed someone to talk to, someone who would give her confidence a boost. In fact, someone like me. I had no idea she was feeling like that and, if she had not voiced the need for help, I would have been on my way thinking all was well. Now she has sent these vibes into the universe, she will get the help she is seeking – ask and it will be given to you. We never know how profitable a few words will be when they fall on the right ears, so it is very important to bring those words out – action from within!

With love I wish you all you wish yourself.
*Remember there is **now and eternity.***
Now is what we have, so start right now!
May God bless you in your search for inner happiness.
Help Yourself To Happiness
Everybody, everywhere seeks happiness, it's true,
But finding it and keeping it seem difficult to do.
Difficult because we think that happiness is found
Only in the places where wealth and fame abound.
And so we go on searching in
'palaces of pleasure',
Seeking recognition and monetary treasure.
Unaware that happiness is just a 'state of mind'
Within the reach of everyone who
takes time to be kind.

For in making others happy,
we will be happy too,
For the happiness you give away,
returns to **shine on you.**
    –Helen Steiner Rice

If, at this moment, you are going through a crisis, know that there is a way through and out of it. We might have reached the same low point but for each of us the way out can be different. But, in the end, all roads lead to Rome!

Recently I was speaking to an old school friend who had suffered severe depression. His physical symptoms had been treated by his doctor but he felt he was at a crossroads in his life. He wanted to find the cause of his illness and treat it. His search brought him to Tai Chi, a concept of bringing balance and control. He found it most helpful, in fact, he soaked it up like magic but, remember, what works for each of us can take a bit of exploring. Most healing therapies are based on similar principles, only the package is different. We can wonder why it works until we are blue in the face but I am quite happy just to let it work. The reason why, well, I think one day all will be revealed and, until then, just follow your heart and listen to your inner voice.

Like food, we need to taste it to know if we like it. So too with alternative medicine. Give it a try and, if it helps, stick with it!

Take this book, for instance. I have been told I am purging myself, getting it all out of my system. All I know is that, with every new day, I am finding it easier to be positive, more in control of the rebuilding of my life. This is not a light-hearted story but a very ordinary person's struggle with life. There was a time that I wouldn't have cared two hoots about the ins and outs of life, I was too busy living it!

Only when I was stopped in my tracks and had time to look around, was I able to get a fuller view of life. A carthorse with blinkers has a very restricted view. It needs a crisis to remove our blinkers. We are then forced to see things previously hidden from us. A crisis forced me to act in a way I would not otherwise have dreamt of doing. I would have plodded on in the same old way. We could ask, who are the lucky ones in life, those who lead a relatively peaceful life or folk, like myself, who have become much more aware of being?

Give No Matter How Insignificant You Might Think Your Gift

Mark 14:3: There came a woman having an alabaster box of ointment, very precious, and poured it on His head.

This made me think, are we pouring the precious gifts we have on anyone's head or are we merely storing up our special thoughts and keeping them for a special time or place? Why not let them out every day, as the woman did who gave to Jesus? She wanted to show her love while he was still there with her. It's no good expressing kind thoughts when a person is dead. We never know when our time on earth is over.

Sometimes we might belittle ourselves, thinking that we have very little, but with God's help a little goes a long way. It may be that the little we do for others is just what they are longing for.

I take great delight in small tokens of love and I can't be the only one. Very often people perform what they consider small, meaningless tasks, for example, calling on a sick neighbour, helping with the shopping, feeding and walking the dog, etc. but to that house-bound person, this is very precious help indeed. At such times, a bond can form and, in the end, our friendship is appreciated as much as our help.

However small we may think we are, however little we have to give, it will be received with great joy somewhere, perhaps, everywhere. The small handful of herbs tossed into a bowl of salad can make all the difference to the taste and enjoyment. As my mother used to say: 'The best things always come in small packages.'

CHAPTER 7

Start With Thought

All of our actions start with thought. It would be wise therefore to prioritise our thinking and make a conscious effort to attune our brain. Once our thoughts are more controlled, the words we speak will correspond and so too will our actions. There is a horrible saying: 'Some people open their mouths without engaging their brain.' I don't like it put that way but it explains what I mean.

At first it seems like a tedious exercise but what training programme isn't at the start? I went into serious training, constantly keeping a check on my thinking and, after a while, it became automatic. Like everything, we need to practise to reap the benefits and we can read about methods until we are blue in the face but the only way to prove if there's any truth in a theory is to give it a go.

I like this little saying: 'Success is the result of good decisions which is the result of experience which is the result of bad decisions.' Experience is a fine teacher.

We, as a family, practise controlling our thoughts, which in turn control feelings, ours and others. By analysing a situation instead of jumping to conclusions, we are better able to reach a truer picture. Also, do not instantly attribute blame. Curb what might have been angry words and don't let words be said in haste.

We can also be very lazy in our thinking, letting others do it for us if we can. I'm sure we are all guilty of not stretching our brains. They are capable of so much more. I once met a man who told me he was finding it hard to concentrate on reading a book. It was as though he had forgotten how. He tended to watch a lot of television. In an effort to correct this, for six months he covered the television with a cloth. If you don't use it, you lose it! It is said that you are what you eat but I say you are what you think. My father always said, 'It is not what goes in through the mouth that defiles man but what comes out.'

Self Hatred

More than half the situations we find ourselves in are not bad but we make them so by thinking. The power of the mind is so strong, we can actually turn a fictitious situation into reality. Look how the mind steps into a dream: it is as real as your waking hours, you can feel it, yet your body lies still. By taking greater command over our thinking, by feeding the brain with positive advice, we are better able to remain more wholesome human beings. The force behind self hatred is so strong, it can turn a fit and active individual into a blob of negativity.

If we hate these wonderful bodies of ours, our bodies will show it. Once we start looking the way we feel, our thinking is confirmed, so how can anyone argue against it?

Sometimes we may have no desire to do anything, or go anywhere, and invariably resort to comfort eating. We gain weight and end up hating the people we have created. If you recognise these symptoms, please say, 'STOP, STOP right now, turn this around and bring about the direct opposite.' The body is so wonderfully made, start to cherish every part of it. Look in a mirror and say, 'I love you.' What you feed into the mind will eventually show itself in the body. How can we love another human being if we don't love ourselves?

When I was in my late twenties, I thought the negative situations in my life were a direct result of God abandoning me. I fell out with Him in a big way! Did I think He was going to wave a magic wand at my command and make life rosy again? But I didn't realise how simple the solution was. It first had to come from me. Not only did I need to ask for help but be prepared to act on the directions given. It took me a long time before I listened but, when I look back, I can see just how many saving ropes were thrown to me.

I heard a little story about a vicar caring for a church in Yorkshire. The Church was low lying and subject to flooding. One day it was particularly bad. The parishioners were forced to leave the Church and begged the vicar to do the same. 'Oh no,' the vicar replied, 'I have spoken to my maker and he will look after me.' The water kept rising. Worried about the vicar the parishioners sent someone in a rowing boat, who pleaded with the vicar to come away from the church. Again he declined assuring them that God would take care of him. The water kept rising, until the vicar was forced to sit on the roof. This time a motor boat was sent to the rescue, but, no, the vicar was not moving. By evening he was clinging to the steeple. This time a helicopter was called in, but to no avail. It kept raining, the vicar drowned and went to heaven. 'I don't understand,' he said to God, 'I have always done my best, served as a missionary, loved my church work. I thought you would have saved me.' God said, 'I don't understand either. I sent a rowing boat, a motor boat and a helicopter!'

Now I examine my life with a fine-toothcomb, not yearly or monthly, but daily. I try not to miss a single clue. I like these words by Froude: 'You cannot dream yourself into a character, you must hammer and forge one for yourself.' A lump of metal or clay remains just that until it is worked on. In all walks of life, you see shapeless people. A professor can repeat great long sentences of worldly knowledge and yet be as shapeless as a bag of potatoes. A gentle gardener, who works among nature for hours on end, can stand out like a giant. When we connect with the true essence of life, we are filled with such zest, like that which bursts from an orange when it's peeled.

Decision

When I have to make a choice, I find indecision saps my energy but, once I make up my mind, I am happier. This shows we are ready to move forward, to act, be positive, take control of our lives. Instead of the mind being here for the body, let the body be here for the mind. Think about it: most of us are constantly looking to satisfy bodily comforts, placing all our energies in staying comfortable and secure in our little spot on earth, but pioneers over the centuries have broken this mould. What drives them to take off? They put their trust in mind power and did not worry so much about the needs of the body.

In Spain, we heard of a custom where young people set off with nothing, only what they stand up in and some warm clothing in case of colder weather. They travel for three months, using only their wits and trusting in God to see to their daily needs. This equips them for dealing with life's difficulties for, if they could survive this, what do they have to fear for the rest of their lives? They form a bond with nature and they see how generous their fellow man can be. Sometimes I feel like having such an experience, just to take off and trust that life will give me all I need. How exciting. What new encounters would I make? What new experiences would I have at first hand? Holidays can give us a little taste of this but they are usually planned. Think of the days when you have just taken off, not knowing where you will end up. Haven't these been wonderful, memorable days?

PART 3

CHAPTER 8

Invisible Network

Learn To Connect With The Invisible Network

I really believe there is an invisible network, or jungle drums of the universe, as I like to call it. Once we open ourselves up, switch on and send out the questions that need answered, before very long a solution will be evident. The thoughts we send out are picked up, analysed and, provided the solution is ripe, the means will be put at our disposal. Some things take longer than others and we have to be alert to what is being sent to us; silence can speak volumes if only we sit and listen.

They say a picture paints a thousand words. Perhaps we will be shown an answer to a problem or given an idea in picture form. Look out for it! Learn to sharpen your awareness, especially if help has been asked for. It will come.

Very often our path will cross with that of a complete stranger, only to find he or she brings us into contact with someone who can shed light on our request. There's the link. At that point, remember to give thanks. This too will be picked up and bring joy to the person who helped you. Likewise, if help is requested of you, do your best to respond and you will be the receiver of thankful joy.

Never Be Disheartened

Even when we are doing all the things we believe to be right, life can take a sudden dive. You are being the good neighbour, you have a positive attitude then, bang, a bombshell drops in your lap. When this happened to me, I wondered, what have I been doing wrong? Then I saw it as an opportunity to practise what I have learned about dealing with what life throws at me. Earlier in my life, it would have floored me.

YES, I now understand that the way around a problem is through it. Short term situations may look impossible but be patient, all will be revealed. Never give up on truth, always have faith and trust that life will look after you; and it will.

Today has been such a day for me. I have done all I can at this moment in time and have asked for help with the problem that faces me. Now I have to be still and wait.

Another new day! I decided there was little I could do physically to alter my present problem so I busied myself with things around the house. I had this terrible urge to get rid of unwanted items in my home. It was as though I was looking for something that was bringing me bad luck. It's strange, I have never had that feeling before. I have never paid heed to such things. I longed for everything to be fresh and new. As I got out of bed so I stripped off all the sheets. This was just the start.

I am a person who loves collecting rubbish of all kinds, thrilled if I can make something out of nothing. However, today my head was full of conflicting thoughts. Why do we cling on to so many material things when people are living in parts of the world where food and shelter are a priority? I could live with half of what I have and still be happy, maybe more so! They say to spring clean and have a good clear out is very purging, well this is exactly how I felt. Like the movies say, 'There would be days like this, Mama said!'

Worry

Worry! They say worry kills, so why do it! We are all guilty of undue worry when actually it achieves nothing. The constant repetition in our head keeps confirming the feeling that we have a problem. Mostly we worry about something that has already happened, or is in the future, robbing ourselves of now. We can never put back the clock, however much we might like to and, even if we could, we would probably do exactly the same. We needed that experience so that the next time we are faced with something similar, we can use it to influence our decision.

If you are worried concerning the future, you know what they say – 'it may never happen' and if it does, deal with it then. I used to write my problems or worries on little pieces of paper and keep them in a 'worry pot'. At the end of each week, I would go through the pot and, more often than not, I would laugh. Did I really write that down? At the time, it was very important but once solved it seemed so trivial. It just goes to prove what a waste of precious time, our now time, worry is. So move away from it. The more we practise this, the easier it becomes.

Panic

Panic - sudden and infectious fear.

Do you panic when things go wrong, say, when an exceptionally high gas bill lands on the mat?

Take the example of a car getting stuck in a bog. The driver panics at the first sight of trouble and revs up the engine but the wheel sinks deeper into the mud. It is more effective to keep a clear head. Always ask for help when in doubt. Sometimes, if we sleep on a problem, it can look quite different in the morning. Never be afraid to talk a problem over with someone. A problem shared is a problem halved.

A Shoulder To Cry On

If someone shares a sad or happy situation with me, I can't help but take it on board. There must be a reason for bringing it to my door. Sometimes I send a card or make a visit with flowers. Other times it may mean giving part of myself in a practical way like, say, shopping, cleaning, or using my car but, occasionally, I get very involved.

This I am pleased to do for I believe that what life has given to me can in some way help another. I would bitterly regret not using the tools I have so, come hell or high water, I give of my very best.

Some may say that this is foolish or wonder why I bother. Sometimes I have tried to quieten the voice in my head by saying I cannot do whatever it is, only to find that the voice gets stronger. In the end I have to act. As I get older, I like to think that wisdom comes to aid me with such missions. Sometimes my dreams are so vivid, showing me a solution to something that has been milling around in my head.

I don't always anticipate the final outcome of a particular plan for you never know if anything will go according to that plan. Sometimes the best way is going with the flow.

The Heart Never Runs Empty From Loving Or The Purse From Giving

More and more life keeps confirming this. If I have something, I am more than happy to share it. This is not necessarily from a material aspect, as much as I would like to. Words cost nothing but let them be worthwhile words, loving and helpful, perhaps a funny story. Laughter is always needed.

We all have something to give away - a smile for instance. Isn't it more pleasant while at, say, the supermarket, to meet folk with smiling faces? Knowledge is something else you can keep giving away and still have.

The funny thing is that the more we talk with other people, the more likely we are to pick up more information. Keen gardeners always have a few plants to give away, and it is lovely to see one's plants in a friend's garden and vice-versa. Years ago, as there were fewer garden centres, it was common practice for people to exchange cuttings and plants. That's how new gardens got started. By giving unselfishly, life has a reward in store.

I love the story of the praying hands. Two friends, both wanting to paint, made an agreement. Knowing it would take money for schooling, one decided to forfeit painting in order to earn the money to keep them both while the other trained in art. One became a great painter, and he painted his friend's hands. Yes, the wonderful, faithful hands which had given so much by staying in the background and working so hard. The painting is the famous 'Praying Hands'. What a tribute to those hands and to his friend.

Never feel that being behind the scenes is an unworthy job. Remember the praying hands. If you ever have the opportunity to praise where praise is due, DO IT. I am sure we all know somebody who works in the background. How nice it would be to surprise them with a little gift or thank-you, perhaps a bunch of flowers. And if you are that one, well done, **the one who is first shall be last and the last will be first.**

Being Positive

Because of our particular circumstances, which involved a legal battle, my husband and I could not completely move on from what had happened. This left us feeling in limbo, as uncertainty loomed all around us. Proving that an injustice had been done took over our life. We no longer thought about doing 'normal' things. All of our energies were channelled into surviving each day and constantly going over legal matters made light-hearted conversation a thing of the past. It was like being in a waiting room or having a death sentence hanging over us.

We knew we hadn't done anything wrong yet the powers that be took a long, long time to settle the matter.

We now have a little more knowledge of how the legal wheels turn but, at that time, we were very naive and never imagined it would drag on for so many years. Only when we started to trust the process of life by looking inside ourselves, did we discover the important things about life and how little we need in order to be happy. It was then we stopped measuring life in material terms.

Finally, we made up our minds that we were going to have a life apart from our legal worries. We would let them run alongside and not let them be the be all and end all of our life anymore. We had nothing more to lose and could only gain. With that attitude, we have gone on from strength to strength and fully believe the truth will be found as someone, somewhere, knows what actually happened. Time and diligence will tell but, in the meantime, we are back in the sunshine and no longer prepared to walk on the shady side. **If we can do it, so can you!**

If We Can Do It So Can You

When a negative thought or situation arises the best thing to do is to turn it around or replace it with a positive one as soon as possible. Auto-suggestion or positive affirmations help greatly. By working on the source of negative situations, we can then turn self doubt into self belief, thus regaining the energy sapped by negativity. By repeating affirmations daily we program our mind to think and act that way. Try these words made famous by Emile Coue:

'Every day in every way I'm getting better and better.'

'I am', are powerful words! When negative, depressing thoughts come to you either from within or without, quickly turn your attention to something happier. Take the power away from the negative! You would not invite criminals into your sitting room so why invite those ugly thoughts into your mind!

Catch Life's Opportunities

When I was at school, I was very taken with cycles: the rain cycle, the reproductive cycle, etc. Now I feel every day, every hour, every minute, is a cycle. That's where free will comes in – when an opportunity affords itself, we can either let it pass or take advantage of it that very minute.

Opportunities will come around again but the actual circumstances will never be quite the same. Once we wake up to the rich treasury just waiting for us to reach out for it, the easier it becomes to actually do it. I hate to miss out on what is presented to me. I want to run with both arms out, eager to catch a new experience. To waste a day because I can't be bothered makes me so sad. No matter how great or small my encounter is, I take the same delight for how often have we set out a little half-hearted only to find we have a smashing time?

As a young girl, I loved the 'Hook a Duck' stall at the fair. Do you remember, you were given a stick with a hook on the end and you won the prize with the number under the duck? Life is like 'Hook a Duck'. We have to keep reaching out. If we stand watching, we will never know what prize awaits us. It's easy to get into the habit of watching other people but there is nothing to compare with the joy of experiencing something first hand. I'm sure we've all said at times, 'Oh, it's all right for other people to do that but I could never do it!' This was how I felt when I first started to drive, then I thought, if other people can do it, so can I, and I did.

On reflection, I can see how I have progressed. How I have conquered depression and restored my energy levels. Now I want to throw that part of my life away and yet, because of those times, a much stronger me has emerged. No suffering is wasted if we put it into perspective and move on. This is not accomplished overnight, as surviving a disaster will remain with us for life, but try to see it as part of our cycle, and trust in the eternal process of life, even after death.

Punishment

We are very good at punishing ourselves and, more often than not, this comes from a guilt complex, from negative thoughts. We all make mistakes, we feel guilty and, with guilt, comes punishment. By playing the guilt tape over and over in our minds, we attract punishment.

Let it go, learn from it but replace it with positive thoughts and actions. Don't dwell on what can no longer be altered. It works. I do it every day.

Rejection

I see rejection in two ways, whether it be from a neighbour, a friend or a member of the family. As we become more aware of ourselves and can see our path in life, we ask exactly what our priorities are. I feel it is then that we slowly change. Perhaps we are not even conscious of that change but others around us will notice. To some, it will seem like a light is shining from within us, if they appreciate truth and honesty. I always remember the saying, 'Birds of a feather flock together,' and I think this is true. I hate to have rigid boundaries and I am always looking to widen my horizons, but I think it is true to say that we tend to seek like-minded people as, with them, we tend to feel happiest.

A path of truth and positive thinking can only make us stronger. Then we have the strength to stand against what we don't want. At one time we may have put up with all kinds of stupid conversation, not wanting to cause upset and we sat on the fence, letting situations upset us rather than cause upset to others.

But the time comes when we can no longer tolerate such behaviour. Bad atmospheres seep into our very soul and, if they are not stopped, be sure they will not produce anything good. In the end, we are not merely helping ourselves but also the person who, if allowed to continue, will think it is acceptable. After all, if we say nothing, they will think we are condoning their behaviour. By being brave enough to stand by our truth, we will help everyone.

As we change, it is inevitable that the world, as we know it, will change. Not everyone will like the new me or you and the first type of rejection may arise. We cannot make that our problem; we have to make choices and so do others. They have the right to walk their own paths and who knows what time will bring. The best friend of truth is time. What we send out today might take time to bear fruit and, in the meantime, our actions or works can cause others to reject us. If our actions are based on truth and love, we must stand firm. Perhaps this is the way we prune some of the dead wood hanging around in our life.

The True Path

The simple, abundant path is not always an easy one to walk, as I am sure other truth-seekers will confirm. What gives me the strength to continue are real life experiences, mine and those I hear about. For example, I saw a chat show on television where three teenagers were determined to rebel against their parents. They wanted sex or a baby. A very brave young unmarried mother stood up and told them what it is like to be a single mum living in a bed sit. She pleaded with the young girls to rethink what they wanted their lives to be like. On that day, the girls showed no sign of being affected and they still intended to carry on in the same old manner.

However, six months later, all three girls were invited back on the programme and admitted that they had heeded the brave young mum's words. I say brave because she had the courage to speak out. They said that, at first, they had not wanted to listen but, nevertheless, they were moved by her story. All three thanked her for standing up in front of thousands to help them and others who might fall into the same pit.

The young mum was invited onto the stage and thanked by the girls who gave her flowers and gifts for the baby. A well-deserved reward as she did not speak out for gain but out of a true desire to help. She was so touched by their thanks. A beautiful moment had emerged because she had been prepared to share her bad experiences with others. Isn't that what it's all about? How wonderful it is that those girls took notice and were prepared to make changes. We never know what a few words of warning and encouragement can do, although it may take time. Eventually we may be thanked for sticking our necks out.

Never be afraid if you feel your experiences can help others. Even if at first it is rejected, we can only keep sending out loving thoughts. Each individual has a right to choose.

I also like the story of the juicy ripe plum, succulent and sweet.

It can be the finest plum in the world but there will still be men who do not like plums. Do we change and become something else in order to be liked by such people? We can remain a first class plum or become a second rate something else. We have the choice to live a lie or seek to be a first class plum.

I used to tell my sons, if you do a kindness for someone, never do it expecting any return. Give freely because you want to. If you don't, don't do it.

Secondly, I believe a higher source is at work. We may suffer rejection, not knowing why, and maybe we are not responsible. Rejection may be one way of taking us away from a potentially worse situation. It could take years before the reason comes to light, if indeed ever. Instead of worrying about the circumstances, try to keep on living a good life, one with heart. If we have Guardian Angels watching over us, who see us living a wholesome lifestyle, I am sure we will be protected. It is hard sometimes just to accept and not try to force a situation our way. I am gradually learning to let go, to let things be.

It would be fantastic to be liked by everyone and to like everyone back but, unfortunately, this is not how life is. Bear in mind the story of my old Dutch lady who said, 'The thief must steal and the murderer must kill. The sooner you stop being anxious and instead practise the lifestyle that suits you the better.'

CHAPTER 9

Trials and Tribulations

Trials and tribulations can actually save us from a path that takes us nowhere. Perhaps, from a materialistic point of view, it looks rosy but, deep down inside, it would not fulfil you. The real you was disappearing into the fluffy carpet! Stepping off that treadmill is very difficult. Often we dream about it but, when it comes to doing it, we get cold feet.

I was forced onto such a path but now, practising what I've written in this book, I really believe I've been saved, plucked out of the mire. It was a hard way to learn of another way of life. But now it feels as though a ton weight has been removed from my shoulders. Joy comes when we are able to accept and not judge. A friend of mine, who has just returned from India, impressed me with what she said about the attitude there of disabled people. They just accept their lot in life - it is their karma this time, no big deal. They remain happy even though they have no legs and have to do jobs like dragging themselves onto trains to brush the floors clean. If only we could put less importance on our physical bodies and instead see ourselves in a more spiritual light.

At the end of this earthly life, we are left only with our experiences. We cannot take a bean with us when we die. True, isn't it? All we collect, our little empires, will be left behind. Yes, we all like home comforts but see them for what they are. Try not to get attached to things that moth and rust can corrode. If we lose out materially, we need to learn to let go, preventing upset and anger eating away at us.

I know people who have lent items to, say, family and friends which, for whatever reason, were not returned. This has resulted in a falling out.

It is better to think that another's need must be greater. Take that attitude and life will return to you much more than you lent in the first place! If only we could shed our pride, our mask and armour, which were probably only put on in the first place to protect us from the competitive world. If we cease to compete, we do not need them. Baring our true selves, we are liberated from all the old chains that held us.

I have found that, by making time for spiritual activities, the materialistic world we live in is enhanced. We are human beings not human doers, although it might not feel like that at times. So why not just be, go with the flow!

How often have we tried to force a situation, causing tension and stress when, if we had just sat back, hey presto, things would have slotted into place, no force needed. Take, for instance, a spot. We always want to squeeze and pick at it, more often than not making it far worse. If we leave it alone it clears up much quicker. Some situations are like that. If after trying to improve a situation we fail, give it the spot treatment. Nine times out of ten it works, leaving us wondering why on earth we fussed in the first place.

How many people go right through their lives with a metal plate in front of their head? A blank sheet of paper, an empty room, an open field, all very scary. Had we better not stay with what we know? After all, what can we write on a blank paper? What should we put in an empty room? What direction to take in an open field?

Are you too scared to try something new?

Choice

The choice is ours and once we are strong enough to face those choices, they can and will transform our lives, turning hate into love, confusion into understanding, poverty into prosperity and much, much more.

Life is for living - let's choose to do just that! They say adversity can make or break us. Once we put the material side of life into perspective, it leaves us free to fulfil a side of us that may have been neglected, for example, growth of mind, spirit and talent. Cultivating our spiritual outlook will act as a guide in such areas.

When I was at a low ebb and my strength to carry on was failing, I felt I had nothing to loose. It is a great pity we cannot realise this before we are at a low point. This wonderful universal energy is around us at all times. Come on, plug yourself in, repair the burnt out fuse, trust that life will give you all you need, and it will!

When life throws us off, we need to find our true centre, in order to regain a purposeful balance. Every one of us needs to find this for ourselves, not by doing things because of other people or competing with others. Look at our own qualities and follow our own heart, mind and spirit.

I really believe honesty to be the best policy. Once we start to twist the truth or hold back our real feelings, it makes our bodies twisted as well, blocking pureness from flowing through. How true the saying, 'Oh what a tangled web we weave when first we practise to deceive.'

Truth is light to carry around and not a burden on us, allowing energy to flow. When blood flows unrestricted though the body, constant healing takes place. Pressure on one spot causes the flesh to break down like a pressure sore. So too with truth. It is healing. Such a way of life is so simple and maybe that is the crux of the matter: are we perhaps looking for a more complicated way?

Life Is But A Dance!

I once read that life and relationships have a pattern like a dance. All you need to do is learn the steps, listen to the music, don't lean back to the last step or press forward to the next. Perfect poise on the beat is what gives good dancing its sense of ease. At first it will be difficult. What makes us hesitate? I think fear. We fear we will make a mistake and then we will do! How can we overcome such fear? By its opposite - love. When we lose ourselves in love there is no room for fear. Living should be an act of love. Go with the music, fall in love with the dance and with your partner, never asking if you are loved in return. Girls, don't look for Mr Right, be concerned with being right yourself! If we fall in love with work, it becomes a pleasure and the more love we bring to everything, the more enjoyable life itself becomes. My father always greeted us in the morning with these words, 'Good morning God's new day, it's good to be alive, a lot of people died last night.' We used to laugh and say, 'Oh Dad, don't say such a thing,' but now I find I'm saying it too!

Hidden Treasures

Life is like the tide, when we see it at low ebb it seems it will never return to the shore. Have faith, it will. Instead, try to find the hidden treasures that can only come to light once the tide is that low. Once we are stripped to the bone, we too can learn a lot about ourselves. Characteristics, normally hidden by the trimmings of life, are revealed. We draw on our own resources. It can come as a real surprise when we achieve things we previously thought impossible.

When I was a little girl, I would often walk on the beach when the tide had gone out, eager to see what had been left behind on the shore. Sometimes an unusual piece of driftwood or a beautiful coloured ball would be waiting to be claimed. I had to keep my eyes open, ready to spot the treasures left by the sea. If I had gone out expecting to find a ball, how disappointed I would have been if I had not found one. So too with life: we can make ourselves unhappy by wanting what we think is ideal, thinking others have it better, when all we need to do is look to ourselves

114

and accept what life gives us.

Learning to find joy in simple pleasures can open up a much more beautiful world, one we never imagined existed. You only need one sun for a sunset or one candle to bring warmth to a dark room. A single rose can radiate more beauty than a vase-full. We can clutter our lives with trivial happenings, have an excess of meaningless experiences, when less of a good thing can actually mean more, in the way it fulfils our soul.

Beauty stands alone. When we look as though we have nothing but our naked selves, no fancy frills, then we are at our most beautiful. We stand with what nature has given us, not striving to attain what the materialistic world classes as beauty!

My family and I were forced to live a very simple life in Spain when things we had previously taken for granted, for instance, running water, were missing. We soon came to respect such things as water and coped with stringent rationing, so glad to have sufficient for that day.

We had no television so instead, in the warm Spanish evenings, the art of conversation lived again. We entertained ourselves, singing, reciting poems and telling jokes. Meal times were more relaxed, with no television to dash off to, no soap opera to keep pace with, and we found our family ties became stronger. A girlfriend of my youngest son, with whom we still keep in touch, longs to return to the Spanish lifestyle. She thinks that was the happiest time of her life. We had very little materially but we were very happy. The house was very sparsely furnished. The kitchen had the bare essentials for cooking and storing food. Despite this, the sun shone every day and the sky was always blue, freely given for all to enjoy.

I find that that time in Spain affects what I do now, right down to simple acts. The other day I lifted a piece of wood in my garden to collect it for the fire but seeing the life which lived beneath it, penny sows, worms and such like, I didn't have the heart to take their home away, so I gently laid it back down. We had some funny changes to deal with daily.

Instead of a milkman, a goat herder came by, milking a little nanny on our doorstep. Couldn't have fresher than that! He would sit awhile, keeping a watchful eye as the herd picked at dried grasses and herbs. All of this taught us how to live life at a slower pace, yet still getting all we needed to live a more satisfying life.

It's funny to think back, if such a lifestyle had been a choice, we would probably have run a mile! Being forced to have less taught me that it was easier to climb with less to carry. Climb in a spiritual sense, I mean, which enhanced other aspects of my life. I am not advocating this as a path for everyone. I'm only telling you of my experience. Maybe that is the secret to life, only to have what is needed, but this is easier said than done.

Realistic Goals

I feel that setting ourselves targets and goals that are out of reach is just as negative as no goals at all.

Sometimes, we are in a rut and have a dream. To be perfectly truthful, we know it is just too far out of reach, but we keep harping on about our dream. 'This is what I intend to do when...' - when never. We can't possibly go down another road because of this 'impossible dream', so it actually is a two-fold block; it stops us from moving on because we stare ourselves blind on what might be achieved, although we are doing nothing to bring this about. While playing this waiting game, we are afraid to try anything new. If only we took an honest look at ourselves and asked how could we change our present situation for the better. Perhaps we have convinced ourselves that a different situation is not for us. How often have you heard, 'I've never been there before, or done that before, so I'd better not go, or do it!' only to find the speaker pleasantly surprised by what the new situation brings to the surface.

For instance, I hated the idea of living in a town house, let alone a town house without a garden. Being a farmer's daughter, I love the idea of land, of animals on the land, of a garden with vegetables. Flowers have their place but you can't eat them!

When circumstances brought about a complete change, and illness hit myself and my husband, it meant heavy gardening was out. We ended up with a paved courtyard right in the middle of town. What do you think? We love it! Now we have more time for other things, such as writing this book. The paved areas cry out for flowers, not vegetables, so I'm learning about potted plants. So much easier than digging and cutting lawns. I also have more time to devote to helping others, which gives me tremendous pleasure.

Very often friends, who still have large gardens, give us fresh herbs, fruit and vegetables, so life without a garden is not as bad as we imagined. Sometimes, as we get older, it is difficult to accept what we now need. We don't want to acknowledge the fact that we can't do as much as we once did.

I worked with the elderly and many a time saw elderly people living in the country but no longer able to drive or in an old house with stairs, now no longer practical. Really a move to town would have been sensible or a bungalow would have been heaven. But instead of seeking to bring this about, very often folk leave it until they can no longer make these decisions for themselves and friends or authorities become involved. So don't let fear or the unrealistic dream stop you from making a change.

You never know what happiness is awaiting you and making a change in direction, giving up on this wonderful dream, might turn out to be the very first step in your new life. To keep on just dreaming – well, we might as well stay tucked up in bed, being comfortable in our dream state! Once we decide to do something, the first step is always the difficult one. As with the first word we write, the first stitch, the first brush stroke.

Once your current situation causes unhappiness, or you find

yourself complaining constantly, the signs are there and it is time to re-assess what you are doing or what is happening around you. Life is very precious, don't just wallow in self pity. Confront your plight and be determined to unblock any part of your life that is making you miserable.

I once heard a man say, 'Well, if I can't do it this way, my way, I won't do it at all.' I immediately thought of him as a very strong tree, so strong that, when a really bad storm hits, he would not be able to bend with the wind but would fall to the ground. Are we so inflexible, so stubborn, that we would rather cut off our noses to spite our faces than to seek a new way? We can all aim for the moon but, on the other hand, don't be disappointed if you only reach the stars. I don't feel this life is all we have – maybe our moon is waiting for us in another lifetime.

I feel and expect life to be exciting and it can be, full of new and wonderful adventures. I try to enjoy every aspect of every day by approaching what I have to do with a good heart.

I also reach out and embrace it with both hands. How excited children are when they stand before a lucky dip, just about to plunge their hands into the sawdust to reveal a surprise package! I have always loved surprises and now I reach into the barrel of life; does the child within ever die? I hope not!

I once saw a very good recipe, I feel it is appropriate here:

THE GOOD LIFE

- Do the best you can, whatever arises.
- Be at peace with yourself.
- Find a job you enjoy.
- Live in simple conditions, housing, food, clothing; rid of clutter.

- Contact nature every day; feel the earth under your feet.
- Take physical exercise through hard work, through gardening or walking.
- Don't worry; live one day at a time.
- Share something every day with someone else; if you live alone, write to someone; give something away; help someone else somehow.
- Take time to wonder at life and the world; see some humour in life where you can.
- Observe the one life in all things.
- Be kind to the creatures.

CHAPTER 10

Being in the Glorious Sunshine

Yes, I feel I have learned how to put the dark days well and truly behind me. I am ready to walk in the sunshine and face new challenges. I have accepted the past and am now able to speak freely about it. In fact, I feel like a spectator standing in the wings looking at a play. Did that really happen to me? My, it seems like a million years ago. Now I am ready for more adventures. I have found myself again and stopped punishing myself.

I heard someone say, 'If you can dream it, you can do it!' Well, I'm having plenty of 'I'd like to do' dreams again. My old confidence is back, along with a blessed assurance that what I really need will come about. No matter what area in my life, personal or business, I have no need to dress anything up. I just have to present myself in a sincere way, stating my reasons for what I want to do quite openly. By talking from my heart; responding with love; not wanting to be clever or to outshine another; looking for a fair exchange and easing a situation rather than pushing, all parties should come out with less scratches. If the exchange is right, the pieces will fit perfectly!

Again I have come to trust, to do my best and to ask for guidance, then wait for the wonderful surprises life has in store for me!

He Who Dares Wins

Yes, we must have courage to go forward, resolved to do what we believe to be right. Never be afraid to follow your heart for, very often, our innermost feelings are correct but fear stops us from acting on them. The chances are that, if we keep denying our true worth and thus blocking the heart path, it will in turn block us, causing pain, disease and disorder of our heart.

Not only will the one who dares win in a material way, attracting their very heart's desires, but also in their health. After all, if we agree with our heart's decisions, it will keep sending out more and more of what is good for us; heart and soul working as one, so to speak.

When we have the opportunity to give of ourselves, that is the moment to grab, that very minute will never come again. From now on, I intend to let the world see me as I really am, win or lose. For the times we appear to have lost might surprise us and do a U-turn. At least we stay authentic.

Sidney Carter wrote, 'No way back. Lean on the future, there if anywhere you walk upon the water. All that was true at first is true at last but there is no way back into the past. But through the future, there if anywhere the miracle must happen.'

The past is the past is the past and that's exactly where it will stay. We have to live now and how we do that will give us good or bad memories in the future. By being conscious of today's actions, the past will read like a good book. I am determined to achieve something every day and, as I have said before, even the smallest deed is important. Visits to family or friends or a newsy letter written to someone make your life worth living. The mornings will have a brightness about them. We will spring out of bed, eager to enjoy the new day, longing to meet its challenges and create new ones!

The Devil Finds Work For Idle Hands

So don't let him find you idle! That does not mean we should be working every hour as relaxation is equally important. This will, however, differ greatly from person to person and that is one thing the past is useful for. Take a look at what works for you. Be prepared to try new ideas - they might be just what you need.

Miracles Happen Every Day

If we could only find joy in the simplicities of life, every day would be a wonderful experience. Who wants to be a millionaire? Yes, we all do from time to time but the reality is balancing the books every month, making ends meet. Let's forget the mundane necessities of life. We have to deal with these, but get them over with as quickly as possible, so that we can get on with the simple joys of being alive. Start to appreciate nature: look at the changes that take place every day in your garden, or local park, or take a leisurely walk in the country.

As a little girl, I walked a mile to and from school each day on a typical country road. In springtime, I picked snowdrops and primroses then watched as the profusion of summer flowers crowded the hedgerows. I ate sloes and hoes, picked baskets of blackberries for those delicious tarts Mum always made. The joys of country living!

Why not bring a few of those memories back? Ask a friend to join you on a country walk and afterwards serve an old-fashioned afternoon tea with bramble jam. Or settle down with that book you've been meaning to read. Give time to yourself. Take a long soak in a scented bath, play your favourite music tape, spoil yourself and enjoy it. Instead of wishing for what you haven't got, enjoy what you have.

Never Be Afraid

Never be afraid to do or say simple things. If worldly-wise men make us feel inferior, just put trust in God. With His help the simplest of deeds will be profound.

In Corinthians 27, we are told God chose the foolish things of the world 'that he might put the strong things to shame.' So we need never be afraid to stand alone, never be afraid to step out of the crowd. Many times I've been hesitant about my writing. I wondered if anyone would ever want to read it or if it is good enough. But I keep telling myself simple things are very often the best. So, as that little black dress is always a winner time after time, more and more I am trying to simplify my life. Lightening the load by caring and sharing, we can ease life for ourselves and others.

I have always had a problem with perfume. When given a beautiful fragrance, I was almost afraid to use it - better keep it for a special occasion. Now I can't wait to release the wonderful scent. What pleasure is there in keeping it in the bottle? It can change my mood for the whole day, awakening my senses of smell as well as making me smell nice. This rule can count right across the board of life. Let's open our precious ointment before it is too late. Give what you've got TODAY.

Do Tell Others

You could say that my experiences have been a sort of life-makeover, the benefits of which I enjoy every day and, being the sort of person I am, I take great pleasure in sharing my good fortune with others. Sometimes a solution is as simple as practising common sense. When, for whatever reason, we just get stuck in a rut, we too easily accept our old patterns or cannot see the wood for the trees.

Opportunities to help another person often present themselves in the everyday workplace. For instance, the other day, I was buying dog food at the pet shop when I noticed that the lady serving me had an injured hand and I asked her if she was all right. 'Oh,' she said, 'I'm accident prone, I'm used to hurting myself.' Before I could stop myself, I told her that she could turn this around and didn't have to accept that blindly. Some people think they are accident prone but, on careful examination, there is another reason. For example, being preoccupied with thinking about things other than what is at hand, stress, anxiety or just day-dreaming causes us to lose concentration for a second and in that moment an accident can happen. I encouraged her to be aware of what she was doing. How many times have you been driving your car and arrived at your destination not remembering the road just travelled? By doing too many things at the same time, you are just waiting for something to go wrong; carry too many plates and one is likely to be dropped.

As we get older, it becomes necessary to write little notes to remind ourselves about little things, like shopping or appointments, but actually it's not a bad idea to do this irrespective of age as it frees the mind and allows us to concentrate on the job at hand.

The shop assistant was so pleased to hear what I had to say and couldn't agree more. She said she had never stopped to think why she was accident prone, or if there was anything to be done about it. I hope I whetted her appetite and she will watch out for such things in the future. I could easily have been about my business and said nothing and I'm sure that, at one time, her comment would have gone over my head, but not so anymore. While on this journey, we might as well extend a hand of kindness. At our wedding, a cousin of mine included in his speech the words by G. K Chesterton, 'Respect those who have travelled before you, honour and respect those who travel with you and, finally, leave a clear and firm imprint in the sands of time for those who follow you.'

C O N C L U S I O N

Like the song says, 'Search for the hero inside yourself.' Remember you are not an average person, you are special.

Motivation is the Key Word

If you are fed up with the way your life is right now do something about it. 10% of people set themselves goals. Out of these 10% only 3% write them down, and those 3% all achieve their goals. Not only do they achieve but they become financially independent - the wealth of this group is more than the rest put together!

From this statistic I learnt that whatever you want out of life, be it improved health, wealth or spiritual growth, first make a written plan.

Once we have made the decision to go forward, doors will start opening for us. Instead of seeing goals as 'What do I want?' see it as 'What can I give to myself?' The secret word is give, this applies right across the board of life. What am I prepared to give to others? We must take responsibility for our actions.

This takes discipline. Remember, the pain of discipline weighs ounces but the pain of regret can weigh tons!

Look for the magic inside yourself, once you find it use it.

My magician son sprinkles waffle dust over the tricks and hey presto, it's magic! Disney shows stars coming from a little girl's feet after visiting Disney Land. Let your particular brand of magic shine for others to see. We are not in a race. We can take the gentle road or use the motorway. What we are after is a way of life, one with quality.

Along with discipline comes the search for the means to bring our dreams to fruition. We need to invest in ourselves, build the skills needed... oil has to be dug for!

I started to practice a positive attitude when I felt I had hit rock bottom, but you don't have to wait until that happens to you. Otherwise you might find yourself saying, this is not for me, I have a little bit further to sink! From the bottom through to the top we need to be positive, approach the ups and downs with the same positive attitude. Once we start to give, we will find we get back what we deserve. Always give thanks for what you have received, thanks to those who help on your path, thanks for all the love that makes this possible, and thanks to the source of love, Almighty God.

Health and wealth are fine for the time we are here, but love lasts forever.

There is little difference between people, but the little difference makes the difference... is it negative or positive?

I wish you well on your particular path and much success in overcoming any difficulties. If something at first appears an impossible situation, you will see that the power of love and your own mind can work wonders. By using the power of the mind, we are able to change the course of our illness, our future, our dreams. Remember, the pessimist looks to the negative but an optimist is always positive, always proclaiming, 'I am succeeding!'

We all have a personal responsibility for our thoughts and actions. Keep visualising a beautiful world. After all, it is far nicer to think of what we want than to keep telling ourselves life will never be any better. The beauty of the fountain comes when it is switched on, so let your fountain spring forth.

Let today see you stepping forth on a golden path. Reach out for the best, that is, the best that's on offer. Never use the measuring stick of another, but learn to feel what you need deep inside your very being. Find your truth and settle for nothing less.

Should you take a few backward steps, in the words of the song, 'Dust yourself off, shake yourself down and start all over again.' In all walks of life, you will come across negative people but try standing up for the positive side of life and soon you will come across wonderful people of like mind. By valuing yourself and your time, other people will soon do the same or get out of your life. If a situation gives off bad vibes, stay away from it and refuse to be drawn in. Guard your good feelings.

Always, I repeat always, think positive, even in a stressful situation. There is always stress in everyone's life but the difference between coping or not depends on our mental approach – if we see problems as obstacles to be overcome. Be practical, take pen and paper and write down positive solutions. Focus on these and see them as already happening. Above all, follow through with positive steps that will bring them about. Start to love yourself, bring your body to the highest level of energy possible and remember the importance of a good diet. After a good spring clean in all areas, you will feel a definite improvement but to what degree will depend on your input. You only get out what you put in!

Once you have tasted that simple, abundant lifestyle, the one that is attainable and is not based on material greed but on a way of life that money cannot buy, you will never ever contemplate looking back. The jewel in your life will be you!

Other publications

Aberdyfi: The Past Recalled – Hugh M. Lewis £6.95
You Don't Speak Welsh! – Sandi Thomas £5.95
Come, Wake the Dragon – Rodney Aitchtey £5.95
Ar Bwys y Ffald – Gwilym Jenkins £7.95

More to follow soon!

For more information about the Dinas imprint, contact Lefi Gruffudd,
General Editor at Y Lolfa

Y Lolfa Cyf., Talybont, Ceredigion SY24 5AP
e-mail ylolfa@ylolfa.com
website www.ylolfa.com
tel. (01970) 832 304
fax 832 782
isdn 832 813